"In the tradition of Tammany Hall and the Jim Crow era, Democrats are still bent on hastily bending and changing election laws to make it easier to wield power. Fred Lucas, a veteran Washington correspondent, details how the Biden-Pelosi agenda is attempting a federal takeover to wipe away states' clean election laws such as voter ID and undermine confidence in elections."

–**Mark Levin**, host of *Life, Liberty & Levin*, #1 *New York Times* bestselling author.

"The left insists every election integrity measure such as voter ID is 'voter suppression' or worse, 'Jim Crow 2.0.' This book by journalist Fred Lucas not only shows why that's wrong, but it details the efforts by Biden, Pelosi, and other Democrats that would federalize and ultimately corrupt the election process."

–**Congresswoman Claudia Tenney**, co-chair of the House Election Integrity Caucus

"Fred Lucas provides a battlespace assessment in the Voting Wars. This is a roadmap for anyone who wants to understand why the Left has poured billions of dollars into transforming our elections into something we wouldn't recognize a decade ago."

–**J. Christian Adams**, President of the Public Interest Legal Foundation

"This is the book Eric Swalwell doesn't want you to read. Fred Lucas takes a clear-eyed look at the 2020 election, what states did right and what they did wrong. If the right people pay attention, maybe 2024 won't be a total mess."

–**Debra J. Saunders**, syndicated columnist and fellow at the Discovery Institute

"Fred Lucas cuts through the name-calling to zero in on both the documented problems in American elections and the effectiveness of recent solutions. Americans tend to agree on a commonsense approach to elections, and purveyors of commonsense will find Fred's book to be loaded easy-to-understand analysis and—critically—solutions to help improve the cornerstone of our republic: our elections."

—**Ken Cuccinelli**, former Virginia Attorney General and former Acting U.S. Deputy Secretary of Homeland Security. National Chairman of the Election Transparency Initiative.

Abuse of Power: Inside The Three-Year Campaign to Impeach Donald Trump

Tainted by Suspicion: The Secret Deals and Electoral Chaos of Disputed Presidential Elections

THE MYTH OF VOTER SUPPRESSION

THE LEFT'S ASSAULT ON CLEAN ELECTIONS

FRED V. LUCAS

Published by Bombardier Books
An Imprint of Post Hill Press
ISBN: 978-1-63758-785-0
ISBN (eBook): 978-1-63758-786-7

The Myth of Voter Suppression:
The Left's Assault on Clean Elections
© 2022 by Fred V. Lucas
All Rights Reserved

Cover Design by Matt Margolis
Interior Design by Yoni Limor

Post Hill Press
New York • Nashville
posthillpress.com

Published in the United States of America
1 2 3 4 5 6 7 8 9 10

To Basia, thanks for the support and encouragement.

Table of Contents

By Kevin Roberts, President of The Heritage Foundation

Frederick Douglass argued that "the liberties of the American people were dependent upon the Ballot-box, the Jury-box, and the Cartridge-box."[1] Conservatives have grown accustomed to political fights over the latter two. Everywhere progressives dominate, from Blue States to college campuses, the right to bear arms and the rights to equal justice and due process are under threat. But historically, even most conservatives have taken the integrity of American elections for granted.

We've all heard stories of urban party machines registering dead folks to vote and frontier elections turning on which candidates offered supporters more rewards. But those tales are handed down as aberrant, rakish folklore—corruption, sure, but of a harmless, victimless sort, better answered with knowing humor than outrage. In a 1958 speech to reporters, then-Senator John F. Kennedy famously jujitsued attacks against his family's enormous wealth by tapping just this vein of political comedy:

> *"I have just received the following wire*
> *from my generous daddy: 'Dear Jack – Don't*

*buy a single vote more than necessary – I'll be
damned if I am going to pay for a landslide.'"*

It is probably not a coincidence that voter fraud is given the kid-gloves treatment by the American media since its most notorious practitioners have always been on the political left: the Long Machine in Louisiana, the Daley Machine in Chicago, the Curley Machine in Boston, the Pendergast Machine in Kansas City, and Tammany Hall in New York. Were voter fraud and machine corruption staples of *conservative* politics, you can bet America's elite institutions would take a less sanguine view of it. Characters like Huey Long, James Michael Curley, and Boss Tweed would be remembered not as Robin Hoods and "rascal kings" but as irredeemable, predatory thugs.

The political press tries to avoid scrutiny of their hypocrisy by adopting a smug schizophrenia on the issue: wryly romanticizing liberals' long, documented, and oft-prosecuted perpetration of voter fraud, while also insisting that it never happens and has never happened and conservatives who say otherwise are lying and racist and trying to steal elections.

Both of these narratives cannot be true. Fred V. Lucas has proven both to be false. *The Myth of Voter Suppression* marshals years of investigative research and reporting into a timely and definitive guide to American election integrity and its enemies.

Lucas traces the Left's history of corrupting Douglass's "ballot box." He removes partisan historians' rose-colored—or, who are we kidding, *blue-tinted*—glasses and uncovers the truth: campaigns of voter fraud were rarely good-hearted mischief. They were almost always racketeering conspiracies against the American people, almost always preying on the rights of poor and minority communities, and almost always in the service of Democratic Party elites.

Those campaigns also never ended. As Lucas demonstrates in the chapters that follow, the Left's election-fraud tactics may have evolved over the years, but their blithe contempt for election integrity is as strong as it ever was.

The good news is today the American people are better informed and more empowered to stop it. Election integrity has become a critical issue in local, state, and national politics. In the wake of various irregularities surrounding the 2020 elections, nineteen states reformed their laws to require voter identification, signature verification for mail-in ballots, clean up old voter rolls, and prohibit ripe-for-corruption practices like ballot harvesting.

The Democrats' multi-million-dollar "voter suppression hysteria industrial complex" has tried to smear all of the above as bigoted attacks against voting rights. But the public is on to the con. Voter ID laws aren't "controversial"—they consistently garner 80 percent support in public opinion polls, including 60 percent of Democrats. Nor does anyone seriously object to updated voter rolls. Both reforms were recommended by a 2005 bipartisan election commission led by Democrat former President Jimmy Carter and Republican former Secretary of State James Baker.

The biggest reason the Left's hysteria has fallen on deaf ears is that *voter fraud still happens all the time!* The Heritage Foundation maintains a database of more than 1,300 prosecuted offenses across the country in recent years. More than a dozen elections were overturned because of fraud.

Faced with this reality, Democrat politicians and their PR firm, the mainstream media, try to change the subject to Donald Trump's accusations about the 2020 election. But it's a trick.

You don't have to believe Joe Biden is an illegitimate president to recognize voter fraud is alive and well, still very much a part of the Democrat Party's political strategy, *and easily restricted by popular, commonsense election integrity laws.*

That's the Left's real fear here: not that election integrity laws are evil, but that they are effective. That's why they prefer to demonize rather than rebut reformers' arguments. Any attempt to fight fraud is met with unhinged attacks about "Jim Crow 2.0,"

"Jim Eagle," and "The Big Lie." (It never occurs to the Democrats hurling these baseless insults that Jim Crow 1.0 *was their idea*.) It's utter nonsense, of course, but also in keeping with the Left's general hypocrisy and dishonesty on these issues.

Their pious outrage about 2020 aside, liberals have no compunction about questioning election outcomes when they lose. Nancy Pelosi routinely called George W. Bush the "president select" after his narrow victory in the 2000 election against Al Gore. Hillary Clinton called Donald Trump an "illegitimate president" throughout his term. The entire Democratic caucus in Congress promoted the "Russia Hoax." Stacey Abrams has made a lucrative career out of pretending she won the 2018 Georgia gubernatorial race. The media never portrayed any of these as a "lie," big or otherwise. Whatever else you may think about Donald Trump, the media's pearl-clutching coverage of his post-election defiance is utterly partisan and performative.

What is sincere is the American people's desire for free, fair elections in which it is easy to vote and hard to cheat.

And to the Left's consternation, that is what the post-2020 state reforms delivered. During the 2022 primaries, states that tightened up their voter ID laws have seen turnout *rise*. On the other hand, deep blue California, whose election rules have gone in the other direction, saw voter turnout fall. The upshot of voter ID, clean voter rolls, and simple, transparent voting procedures seems to be more voters and increased trust in the process.

The real question is, *why does the Democratic Party oppose free, fair, and credible elections?*

The Myth of Voter Suppression answers that question. It is more than an eye-opening history or a tightly-argued policy brief. It is a concise, accessible, indispensable handbook to the most important challenge facing American democracy today.

War Over Elections

Eric Swalwell generally seems to serve no higher purpose in public life than booking appearances on cable news programming and frequently providing comic relief to critics with a messy personal life. Though to kick off 2022, the California congressman cranked up alarmism about the midterm election. It would be America's last election, he warned.

"I'm worried that if Republicans win in the midterm elections, that voting as we know it in this country will be gone. They're already putting as many barriers to the ballot box as possible in Arizona, Florida, Texas, Georgia. And on the other side of the finish line, they're putting in place processes where they could reverse the outcome even if we crawl through glass and run through the fire to get to the ballot box," Swalwell, a Democrat, told Chris Hayes on MSNBC. "And so if they are able to win the House, the damage they could do to permanently make it difficult to vote and just alter the way that we participate in the democratic process could be irreversible. This is not only the most important election. If we don't get it right, it could be the last election. Because they're also putting in place what I believe is a way to make sure that Donald Trump wins with what they're doing across state legislatures to allow them to reverse the outcome and the electoral college."[2]

Swalwell didn't bother explaining how Arizona, Florida, Texas, and Georgia were putting up "barriers to the ballot box." He certainly didn't explain how the GOP would "reverse the outcome" of elections. He was on MSNBC, so he of course knew he wouldn't have to explain or get any follow-up questions from Hayes. He either knew this isn't true, or he's so committed to his party's talking points that he doesn't care.

Though Swalwell's warning about being in the abyss of tyranny seemed rather unhinged, he was essentially following the script Democrats have floated at least since roughly 2006, when his party first challenged the constitutionality of Indiana's voter ID law. The Supreme Court, in a 6–3 ruling, upheld ID law, asserting states have an interest in protecting their elections.[3]

The phrase "voter suppression" is itself politically-loaded, intended to be overly broad and lacking any legal foundation, as this book explains later. The hysteria behind the myth of rampant voter suppression has been mainstreamed because of institutional support and turned into a strategy for building an old-school political machine similar to those run by big city bosses—only this time taking it national.

With clearance from the Supreme Court, mostly Republican-leaning states and many purple states began adopting voter ID and other election integrity measures, such as removing the names of deceased individuals from voter registration rolls.

Such measures generally had popular support, as thirty-five states now have voter ID requirements. However, Democrats and nonprofit allies such as the Brennan Center for Justice, a legal think tank at New York University, Democrat super lawyer Marc Elias, and other key figures and institutions launched a legal jihad and invoked voter suppression—occasionally even trying to scare Americans about "Jim Crow 2.0," a reference to one of the worst eras in American history. The fact is that if most Democrats had their way through enacting federal legislation to scrap election safeguards, the country would be closer to a Tammany Hall 2.0.

Evangelist of the Suppression Religion

The voter suppression hysteria industrial complex was entrenched with establishment political and media backing, but it was not strong or believable without a compelling messenger. Enter Stacey Abrams, a charismatic Democratic leader in the Georgia state legislature who talked about the dangers of voter suppression during her 2018 campaign for Georgia governor against Republican Secretary of State Brian Kemp. She ran a strong campaign but lost by fifty-five thousand votes to Kemp.

We've heard certain politicians and pundits sound repulsed that a losing politician would refuse to accept defeat and make a string of unfounded allegations of a rigged process that could risk undermining public confidence in the entire electoral process. That's how Democrats describe Donald Trump's "Stop the Steal" crusade after losing the 2020 election.

Two years earlier, Stacey Abrams took that same stance after losing the state of Georgia to Kemp by about five times as many votes as Joe Biden defeated Trump by in the Peach State. Yet, much of the mainstream media says Trump's insistence that he really won in 2020 is a threat to democracy while casting Abrams as a courageous champion for voting rights.

Abrams, since that election loss, gave the Democrats a powerful spokesperson that they didn't have with the Brennan Center and a cadre of partisan election lawyers. The Left went from uninspiring legal eggheads to the inspiring oratory of Abrams about the rigged system that Republicans are imposing on America. She turned her election loss into a national empire, establishing a network of nonprofits.

Abrams became the pastor who spread the religion of large-scale voter suppression and labeled a 2021 law in her state that expanded a voter ID requirement to absentee ballots as being "Jim Crow 2.0." Abrams gained fame in the Democratic Party that she may not have attained had she been elected governor by insisting without evidence that she is the rightful Georgia governor had she not been robbed through voter suppression. Evidence? The Republicans probably suppressed the evidence along with all the votes that would have made her governor.

When Did Election Security Become Partisan?

A back-bencher congressman talking about the last American election and a sour grapes candidate who lost a governor's race are one thing.

One might expect more from the president of the United States. In Statuary Hall at the US Capitol, marking the one-year anniversary since rioters stormed the seat of government on January 6, 2021, President Biden was expected to offer a somber tone. Instead, he used it to deliver red meat for the Democrat base, largely attacking Trump and repeating broad claims of state voter suppression without naming states nor explaining how such states suppressed anyone's vote.

"Right now, in state after state, new laws are being written—not to protect the vote, but to deny it; not only to suppress the vote, but to subvert it; not to strengthen or protect our democracy, but because the former president lost," Biden said, referring to Trump. "Instead of looking at the election results from 2020 and saying they need new ideas or better ideas to win more votes, the former president and his supporters have decided the only way for them to win is to suppress your vote and subvert our elections. It's wrong. It's undemocratic. And frankly, it's un-American."

In 2021, there were nineteen states—including those referenced by Swalwell—that passed election law reforms, which this book will detail later. In summary, most of the laws added a voter ID requirement to absentee ballots—meaning voters needed to provide either a driver's license number or the last four digits of their Social Security number in the absentee ballot application form. Generally, the laws codified a return to pre-COVID-19 voting procedures. Many of the measures also restricted ballot harvesting, which is the practice of allowing political operatives to game the absentee voting process that has been frequently used to intimidate voters. Some states opted to do a better job of cleaning voter registration rolls to remove the names of the deceased or those who moved out of the locality or state. A few states changed the makeup of state election boards.

It wasn't that long ago that such state laws would have had broad national consensus. In 2005, the bipartisan Commission on Federal Election Reform, co-chaired by former Democrat President Jimmy Carter and former Republican Secretary of State James Baker, called for states to increase voter ID requirements, expressed skepticism about mail-in and absentee voting, and called for a halt to ballot harvesting for states to clear dead people off the voter registration lists, allow authorized election observers to monitor ballot counting, and to ensure voting machines work properly.[4]

A war over elections has ensued in which to some degree both sides are unwilling to accept an election outcome and make pre-Election Day excuses for losing to discredit the other party's victory and tag the winner with a taint of illegitimacy. It did not have to be this way. The Carter-Baker commission report provided a bipartisan road map for election reforms that could have increased the public's confidence in the integrity of the vote. Instead, when some states dared to act on the reforms that could have instilled confidence in elections, Democrats viciously attacked the reforms to stir more mistrust of the electoral process.

In 2021 and 2022 this boiled over into a battle between Congress and states. As states passed more anti-fraud measures, US House and Senate Democratic leaders have sought to undo those measures and expand voting to, in fact, make it easier to cheat. In response to Republican-led state efforts, congressional Democrats all but declared a national crisis and threatened to eliminate the Senate filibuster, pushing federal laws aimed at nationalizing election law and nullifying existing state election laws. More absurdly, Democrats are calling these proposals "voting rights" bills. That's clever labeling. Who could be against voting rights? Even better labeling, Democrats brought up the "For the People Act" in early 2021. Apparently, anyone opposing such legislation is against the people.

Such legislation is not in the tradition of the 1993 National Voter Registration Act and the 2002 Help America Vote Act, both of which were built on the success of the 1965 Voting Rights Act. All three of these laws were broadly bipartisan. By contrast, Democrats in Congress have sought to use their narrow majority for a partisan power grab.

The mammoth "For the People" bill would eliminate most state voter ID laws, expand ballot harvesting, mandate Election Day voter registration, and require no-excuse absentee voting in all states. In many respects, this would lock in the advantages Democrats reaped from the COVID-19 election rules. This same law also would have required states to appoint unelected bureaucracies to draw up congressional districts based on the view that Republicans benefit more than Democrats from gerrymandering.

Republicans called this proposal the "Corrupt Politicians Act." The bill hailed as "voting rights legislation" in the pages of the *New York Times* and on MSNBC passed the House but died from a Senate filibuster.

Democrats proposed a more scaled-down version in the "Freedom to Vote Act" that imposes national Election Day voter registration, automatic voter registration, and absentee voting requirements on states, as well as the gerrymandering proposal. The John Lewis Voting Rights Advancement Act (named for the late civil rights hero turned Georgia congressman) would require federal approval of state election law changes. These bills similarly passed the House and were stalled in the 50–50 Senate, with a functioning Democrat majority after the 2020 election relying on the tie-breaking vote of Vice President Kamala Harris.

Free and Fair Elections in Peril?

The United States of America that has done so much to spread democracy around the world, the nation that Ben Franklin remarked was "a republic if you can keep it," is divided regarding the trustworthiness of elections themselves. In a country polarized along so many other issues, both parties express fear that free and fair elections are in peril. They vociferously disagree on both the diagnosis and the cure.

Democrats affirm, some with hysterical flair, that voter suppression is the problem. However, legitimate and adjudicated cases of eligible voters prevented from voting are at best miniscule, and when caught have usually been prosecuted. Vote denial, voter intimidation, and voter dilution are illegal. So, when, for lack of a better term, "suppression" occurs, it violates federal and most state laws.

After Abrams called the 2021 Georgia law "Jim Crow 2.0," and President Biden upped the ante by calling the Georgia law "Jim Eagle," corporate giants wanted to out-virtue signal one another to show how opposed they were to the election law, including Coke, Patagonia, Delta, Mailchimp, and notably Major League Baseball.

Comparing the actual Georgia law—ID for mail-in voting, restrictions on ballot harvesting, and putting ballot drop boxes in statute—with the hyperbole about the law is rather astonishing. The same could be said of Texas, Florida, Arizona, Iowa, and other states that passed election reforms that Democrats slandered as racist.

"Jim Crow" can be cheap rhetoric when aimed at southern states—or even red states. Joe Biden's own state of Delaware has more restrictions than Georgia on early voting, and so does New York. Even the Brennan Center for Justice—which specializes in racial demagoguery on voting laws—was at least consistent enough to call the New York state voting system, "the worst in the country." A UC Irvine election law scholar said if New York "were a southern Republican state, there would be protests and calls for businesses to boycott [the state], because it's that terrible." [5]

In fact, it was in New York—not Georgia, Alabama, or Mississippi—where 125,000 registered Democrats in Brooklyn were dumped from the rolls ahead of the hotly contested Democratic presidential primary between Hillary Clinton and Bernie Sanders. This occurred during what was supposed to be a routine removal of ineligible voters, but the *New York Times* reported at the time, "Amid an investigation into the New York City Board of Elections and widespread complaints about voters being turned away from the polls on Tuesday, it now seems likely that many legitimate voters were mistakenly disenfranchised." [6]

Still, New York may have the worst of both worlds. In the absence of a voter ID law, those other New York restrictions don't seem to make the ballots there more secure. More on that later.

Ballot Wars

The stated intent of the 2021 state election reforms is to make it easier to vote and harder to cheat. Even the skeptical view that these laws help Republicans win is rooted in the fact that GOP lawmakers have reason over decades to defend against fraud. Moreover, evidence is lacking that any such measures suppress anyone's vote.

The fact is Democrats used COVID-19 to implement much of the voting agenda it had pushed for decades and to normalize what had previously been shady voting behavior.

A war is being fought in this country. The battlefields are Congress, in state legislative chambers, and in the courts. At stake are American democracy and the integrity of elections. The two warring narratives overlap—voter fraud vs. voter suppression—and both have historical legitimacies. But regarding the current times, only one narrative has facts to support it. The other has only emotion and inflammatory rhetoric.

The war is theoretically not about who wins and loses, only how the game is played. But of course, the war is about who wins and loses. The Left says voter suppression is a big problem. The Right says voter fraud is a big problem.

Thus, anytime a law to prevent voter fraud is proposed, left-wing politicians and pressure groups howl about voter suppression and dredge up an ugly era of American history. This is not rooted in fact, but it is an excuse for opposing what polls show the vast majority of Americans of all races support—a trustworthy election system.

Neither voter fraud nor voter suppression presently poses an existential threat to the republic. But we do know elections have been stolen or attempted to be stolen through fraud. While stubborn facts weigh heavily with the threat being voter fraud, the ugly history of voter suppression in America still makes the mere words a salient and emotional talking point that is more effective than any evidence Republicans might tout.

Going back to the days when Aaron Burr established Tammany Hall, voter fraud has been part of the Democratic Party's playbook. They are not uniquely guilty, as Republicans have done many underhanded things over the decades. But Democrats tend to be better at fraud. The war today is not so different from the machine politics era of Tammany Hall in New York, the Daley machine in Chicago, the Pendergast machine in Kansas City, and various machines across the country with the single-minded priority of getting out their vote by almost any means necessary.

Eventually, voter suppression would also be key to the Democratic Party's playbook as well until it became an unsustainable strategy. Jim Crow was entirely about racism, but it was rooted in a long-standing Democratic Party tendency to twist voting laws and procedures as a means of winning elections. That was the commonality the Jim Crow laws of the South had with the political machines in northern industrial states. It is also the commonality of what Democrats are pushing in Congress today with the "For the People Act" and other Orwellian-named proposals intended to maintain a permanent majority.

In the past, reformers—who identified as progressives—battled the political machines, fought in favor of the secret ballot, and fought against voter intimidation and voter fraud. The problem today is that many self-styled reformers and progressives on the left are in league with modern-day machines actively pushing laws to undermine the secret ballot and make voter intimidation and voter fraud easier—and are using race as the cudgel to do so.

PART ONE

Chapter 1

The Interwoven History of Fraud and Suppression

Sen. Joe Biden explained his opposition to a proposal floated by the president of his own party when Jimmy Carter backed Election Day voter registration in 1977. The first-term Delaware senator wrote, a "reservation I have and one that is apparently shared by some of the top officials within the Department of Justice is that the president's proposal could lead to a serious increase in vote fraud."[7]

Today, Democrats would label such sentiments as voter suppression.

Over a decade, Biden's concern about fraud didn't wane, as he teamed with then-freshman Sen. Mitch McConnell of Kentucky for the bipartisan Anti-Corruption Act that passed in 1989. Biden said, "Current law does not permit prosecution of election fraud…This bill makes it a federal offense to corrupt any state or local election process."[8]

His metamorphosis on this matter appears to have occurred while serving as vice president in the Obama administration that sued states for enacting voter ID laws and clearing the names of the dead from voter registration lists. In a 2014 speech at Allen University in South Carolina, Vice President Biden rhetorically asked, "Why, without any proof of voter fraud, have 81 bills been introduced in state legislative bodies…to make it harder for people to vote?"

Biden almost surely knew better than to say, "without any proof of voter fraud." He simply parroted the party line that any anti-fraud measures—even those he might have supported a decade earlier—were nothing more than voter suppression.

By the time he was president, as his party was claiming a new Georgia election reform would suppress voting, Biden even said, "This makes Jim Crow look like Jim Eagle. I mean, this is gigantic what they're trying to do, and it cannot be sustained."

It's not entirely clear what that even means other than eagles are bigger than crows, thus the Georgia law must be worse than the original Jim Crow era. That evidently meant that a state law requiring ID for absentee ballots was worse than poll taxes, literacy tests, and fire hoses that existed in the days when Democrats George Wallace, Bull Connor, and James O. Eastland tried to prevent Blacks from voting.

Perhaps awkwardly, Biden was actually one-upping the party line on the Georgia law.

After Gov. Brian Kemp signed the Georgia election reform into law, which included requiring voter ID for absentee voting, bans on ballot harvesting, and restructuring the state board of elections, the self-proclaimed rightful governor of Georgia, Stacey Abrams, framed the talking points for the party.

"Now, more than ever, Americans must demand federal action to protect voting rights as we continue to fight against these blatantly unconstitutional efforts that are nothing less than Jim Crow 2.0," Abrams said.

Abrams emerged as the leading spokesperson for the voter suppression hysteria industrial complex made up of various politicians and interest groups on the left peddling scare tactics and smears, trying to convince the public America is stuck in the 1870s.

Sen. Elizabeth Warren, D-MA, didn't want to be left out and tweeted of Kemp: "The Republican who is sitting in Stacey

Abrams' chair just signed a despicable voter suppression bill into law to take Georgia back to Jim Crow."

The party of Jim Crow—the Democrats—can't stop talking about Jim Crow. They simply found a new way to play the race card for electoral advantage. The Democrats are accusing Republicans of trying to steal elections and attack democracy with most of the same predictions they made since state voter ID laws became popular in the early 2000s, none of which came true. In reality, it has been Democrats who have been behind the vast and shameful history of both voter fraud and voter denial (or suppression, if you prefer) in American elections, which generally have interwoven legacies.

First, it should be noted the term "voter suppression" is rather vague. It is illegal under the 1965 Voting Rights Act to engage in voter intimidation or to act in a way threatening someone trying to cast a vote. Vote denial is illegal under federal law, which could include a law aimed at preventing a legally eligible voter from exercising his or her constitutional right to vote. Vote dilution, which is an intentional effort to dilute the votes of one group of people, is also illegal. It's difficult to say any of these are honestly occurring in an institutionalized and consistent way from a state or local government. Although ballot harvesting scams—to be detailed later—certainly involve voter intimidation. There have also been campaign workers and private organizations that have acted in illegal ways to prevent eligible voters from voting—that were in most cases prosecuted.

As J. Christian Adams, a former Justice Department attorney now president of the Public Interest Legal Foundation, wrote in 2020: "You could search long and hard in the lawbooks containing the United States Code and nowhere will you find one single law that mentions voter suppression. That's because voter suppression is a myth. It is a term made up to smear perfectly legal activities—like voter ID laws—by suggesting it is illegal." He continues, noting that so-called voter suppression "is a term that seeks to blur the line between the legal and illegal in order to taint and smear Constitutionally protected activity, or perfectly legal state laws."[9]

Real vote denial and voter intimidation were rampant after the end of Reconstruction until 1965, when Democrats imposed Jim Crow to manipulate voting laws to gain an electoral advantage. Today, Democrats invoke Jim Crow to manipulate voting laws to gain an electoral advantage.

Invoking is certainly better than imposing. But after Jim Crow laws became impossible to enact, Democrats had to pivot on strategy—while continuing the tried-and-true formula of identity politics.

Democrats are not just the party of Jim Crow but also the party of Tammany Hall. And to solve this supposed rampant suppression problem, Democrats in Congress are pushing Tammany-style legislation with feel-good names such as "For the People Act" to establish a legal structure for making fraud easier and installing long-term majorities.

It wasn't always the case, but today the competing narratives tend to be the Right's concern about voter fraud and the Left's concern about voter suppression. The two evils are not mutually exclusive. On the contrary, twin evils tend to walk hand in hand. Voter suppression was one form of fraud because this improperly skewed election outcomes. Likewise, fraud is a form of voter suppression because phony or ineligible votes ultimately cancel out or dilute the ballots cast by eligible voters.

Tammany Hall, and all the smaller corrupt machines spread throughout the United States, had the same ultimate mission as the bigots running the Jim Crow elections in the South. The mission for both was warping the election law and procedures to ensure Democrat victory. The machine Democrats were best known for fraud, while the Democratic Party's Jim Crow policies are most known for mass voter suppression, violence, and intimidation of African Americans. But the dastardly southern deeds also included methods identical to the northern Democrat machines, such as ballot theft, burning ballots, illegal arrests on Election Day, importing voters who lived outside the precinct, and recording votes cast by dead or fictional people, according to US District Judge Lynwood Smith, who did a report in 2011 on the Jim Crow election practices.[10]

While fraud and suppression exist as competing narratives, it's entirely inaccurate to either presume we must tolerate some fraud to avoid suppression or tolerate some suppression to avoid fraud. Common sense election integrity laws can prevent both. But the party that has opposed clean election laws since the 1800s demagogues proposals today. Voter suppression (though it once plagued America) is nothing other than a talking point in modern times.

There is also significantly less fraud today than in decades past under the reign of Tammany and other machines. Fraud may only rarely make a difference in the outcome. But, as this book later explains, voter fraud has made a difference in modern times often enough to take seriously. Even if election fraud doesn't steal an election, it is stealing votes, canceling out the weight of legitimate votes casts—thus disenfranchising eligible voters. In that sense, fraud is the only provable suppression that is occurring today.

Battle for the Secret Ballot

Among the earliest advocates of election integrity was Sen. Matthew Quay, a New York Republican. He was battling Tammany Hall, which was gunning for him.

Because of Tammany Hall tactics, there were substantially more "votes" than voters. In 1844, New York recorded fifty-five thousand votes even though there were just forty-one thousand eligible voters.[11] From 1868 to 1871, the New York City voting total was 8 percent higher than the entire voting-eligible population because of Tammany's proficiency with fraud, Hans von Spakovsky and John Fund explained in their book, *Our Broken Elections*.[12]

So, in 1888 Quay's campaign canvassed all of New York City—gaining a complete record of all residents. This allowed him to deter fraudulent voting.[13]

Today, Democrats routinely call seeking an accurate accounting of eligible voters "suppression."

In the 1880s through the 1920s, numerous election law changes were made. The public became fed up with corruption, and reforms often associated with the Progressive Era went into place. States gradually started passing laws requiring voters to register before they just showed up at the polls. Also, the secret ballot was instituted—replacing voice voting, or the casting of color-coded ballots handed out by political parties. All these reforms would by definition make it more difficult to vote—thus easily fitting the Left's modern-day broad definition of suppression. The changes were bad news for Tammany Hall, as turnout fell by 15 percent after the anti-fraud measures went into effect.[14] Sometimes it's good when the voter "turnout" is lower.

Specifically, the hyperbole and clashing concerns about voter fraud versus voter suppression closely resemble the battle for the secret ballot.

In the early days of the republic, elections were decided through voice voting—typically at town gatherings. So, for those who worry Thanksgiving dinners or neighborhood cookouts can be difficult to navigate when politics come up—or fret that cancel culture could cost someone their job for the "wrong" opinion—imagine a time when all your neighbors knew exactly how you voted.

It wasn't always safe to vote a certain way when everyone knew about it. The upside was that political campaigns in large cities would sponsor Election Day parties with free food and booze available, as well as torchlit parades. In rural locations, Election Day frequently coincided with farmers' market days. Politics was a big party and a public spectacle.

When it wasn't voice voting, then political parties distributed color-coded party "tickets," or a slate of candidates handed out to voters to drop in the ballot boxes. While it might be better than having to shout your vote, that bright colorful preprinted party ballot was always a dead giveaway to election officials who the vote was for.[15]

The voters would sometimes drop the colorful ballot into a clear glass ballot box—so it was often obvious who was winning.[16] Party machines hired people known as "peddlers," "hawkers," or "bummers" to hand the ballots out at the polls. [17]

This accepted method began to change in the middle of the nineteenth century but—similar to the common sense ID laws of today—those changes did not come easy either. The intellectual predecessors to groups such as the Brennan Center for Justice and Fair Fight Action—meaning the political machines that didn't want their favorable system to change—provided staunch opposition. They launched extraordinarily similar arguments against a secret ballot that their successors use today against voter ID, clean voter rolls, and curbing ballot harvesting.

It wasn't until 1856 that some localities in the United States first adopted what was called the Australian ballot system. Today, it's just known as the secret ballot. The mates down under pioneered this system to combat election fraud and corruption.[18]

By 1871, California—not quite there yet on the Australian model—pushed a precursor to secret balloting with a state law requiring party tickets be printed in a standard way, the same color and on similar paper. The voter could fold the party ticket of his choice before dropping it in the ballot box.[19]

In 1888, Massachusetts was the first to adopt a secret ballot statewide.[20]

It might seem puzzling today to understand why anyone would object to a secret ballot. In that era, there was plenty of resistance to such laws. The publicly stated reason was—you guessed—voter suppression, for lack of a better term.

Illiteracy rates were high in the 1800s, and either voice voting or color-coded ballots for a party's slate of candidates arguably made the enfranchisement broader than entering a private voting booth, closing the curtain, and selecting from a menu of competing party nominees. A secret ballot was what would be called today a "restrictive" form of voting. There was no one for a voter to talk to or get advice from. This had a straight-up disproportionate impact on the poor who had higher illiteracy rates, so went the argument of secret ballot opponents. Thus, jurisdictions jumping on this secret ballot fad were trying to suppress the votes of the poor.[21]

As it turned out, the secret ballot did not produce the horrifying mass voter suppression that entrenched machine politicians warned about.

Nevertheless, the argument might not be settled as you would think. Some on the left blame the secret ballot for allowing Donald Trump to win in 2016. The *Washington Post* ran an op-ed in 2017 that demanded a return to public voting. "Given that some of what Trump said during or before the campaign was so racist, xenophobic and misogynist, naturally voters might not want to be associated with it. The secret ballot provided them the luxury of voting for him anyway." The column continues, "If a candidate acts in indefensible ways—and one must recall that throughout the campaign even the GOP leadership often refused to defend Trump—it is the voters who ultimately bear responsibility for defending him. The secret ballot allowed many of them to get away with never having to do so."[22]

This is not a mainstream view on the left—yet. But one of the nation's largest newspapers published it, and some of the congressional proposals in the election nationalization bills that would take a wrecking ball to the most basic election security standards seemed unthinkable just a few years ago.

Voting Rights Act a Smashing Success

A return of Jim Crow laws—at least as applied to voting—could only legally occur if there was no federal Voting Rights Act, and too many Democrats seem to pretend that's the case.

What's wrong with accepting—indeed celebrating—that the 1965 Voting Rights Act has been an incredibly successful law? Moreover, if the Supreme Court has determined more recently that a certain provision of the VRA is no longer relevant—because of higher voter registration and voter participation rates from African Americans—that should be another sign of success.

That said, it's impossible to ignore the reprehensible history of discrimination in America that kept the country from living up to the goals of the Declaration of Independence and the Constitution.

To some degree, America kicked off under a legal regime of voter suppression at a time when only land-owning white males were generally allowed to vote. The 1820s movement toward Jacksonian democracy opened the doors of self-governance even to white males who didn't own land, which was at the time a big step.

Importantly, women were disenfranchised until 1920. To be sure, it was a tough struggle. But after the Constitution specifically recognized their right to vote, that was pretty much the end of it. By contrast, Black Americans met immense resistance, primarily from state and local governments in the South, to prevent them from voting.

What makes the one-hundred-year post-Civil War disenfranchisement of African Americans different from the disenfranchising that preceded the Jacksonian era, or even that which preceded women's suffrage, is that the Fifteenth Amendment made voting a constitutional right for all American men, at least, but the right was nevertheless denied to Black Americans in many states at an institutionalized level.

It was the 1876 election, marred by fraud and suppression in southern states, that unraveled Reconstruction in the South. Even today it's basically impossible to know who the rightful winner was between Republican Rutherford B. Hayes and Democrat Samuel Tilden. Tilden won the popular vote, but that was likely an illegitimate count. The post-election standoff was decided by the Compromise of 1877, where Republican lawmakers reached a deal and peeled off just enough Democrats to vote to certify Hayes's victory on the grounds the Republican administration would end Reconstruction in the South. Hayes honored his word and has been pilloried for it in history. But it was a near impossible situation. Had Tilden become president, matters would have almost certainly been far worse, and the Jim Crow South would have likely had federal support rather than apathy.

The Jim Crow South was about more than voting and essentially gave legal impunity to white mobs to commit violence against Black Americans. But preventing the Black vote was key to maintaining white supremacy. It first kept Black candidates out of office and ensured that political candidates wouldn't lend an ear to the concerns of Black constituents. Also, in most states, jury pools are drawn from voter registration lists. Maintaining all-white juries was key in the Jim Crow South to ensuring that violent supremacists participating in lynching and other violence would be acquitted.

Literally a full century after the end of the Civil War—1965—a bipartisan majority approved the Voting Rights Act, and southern Democrat President Lyndon Johnson, who as a member of Congress mostly opposed civil rights, signed the bill. This came after he signed the landmark 1964 Civil Rights Act, which also had massive bipartisan support.

When the Civil Rights Act of 1964 passed, 80 percent of House Republicans and 82 percent of Senate Republicans supported it. That's compared to 61 percent of House Democrats and about two-thirds of Senate Democrats who supported it. The numbers for the 1965 Voting Rights bill were 82 percent of House Republicans in support and 78 percent of House Democrats. Meanwhile, 94 percent of Senate Republicans and 73 percent of Senate Democrats supported the Voting Rights Act.[23]

Notably the bipartisan Voting Rights Act of 1965—that clearly tackled a much larger problem than any perceived today—was twelve pages long, while the extremely partisan "For the People Act," aka, the "Corrupt Politicians Act," was eight hundred pages long. The follow-up "John Lewis Voting Rights Advancement Act" is 120 pages long.[24, 25]

The Real Jim Crow

Just as it's distasteful to compare certain unpleasant political issues to the Holocaust or slavery, the same should be true of comparing almost anything to the Jim Crow era, which was literally an apartheid system in several states, based on segregation and violence. Specific to voting, this included poll taxes that placed a financial penalty on Blacks that wanted to vote, grandfather clauses requiring ancestors to have been eligible to vote, whites-only primaries, arbitrary literacy tests, and sometimes absurd requirements to accurately guess the number of jellybeans in a jar or the amount of suds in a bar of soap.

Putting aside what is or isn't acceptable political hyperbole, Jim Crow has a literal historical legacy. Beyond voting laws, other overtly racist laws restricted employment and educational opportunities for Black Americans. Schools, parks, recreation facilities, water fountains, restrooms, and other public buildings routinely were segregated.[26] The Jim Crow era included domestic terrorist activity by the Ku Klux Klan, which committed violent and deadly acts against Blacks. Columbia University historian Eric Foner called the Klan the "military force serving the interests of the Democratic Party." When racist laws couldn't stop African Americans from exercising their constitutional rights, white supremacist mob violence did.

From 1865 to 1900, there were 262 disputed House elections—most of which occurred in the old Confederacy. The disputes were usually cases of election fraud, violence, and voter intimidation.[27]

This was the real Jim Crow era—not the hyperbole used by Stacey Abrams and the Left about showing an ID to vote.

Voter Turnout amid Supposed Suppression

As a practical matter, suppression is a difficult argument, but it's one the Left has hammered heavily since 2011 after newly-elected

Republican state legislatures began enacting voter ID laws across the United States.

President Biden's Assistant Attorney General for Civil Rights Kristen Clarke claimed that states are "making it harder to register to vote." The Census Bureau numbers disagree. In 2020, voter registration reached 72.7 percent, more than the 70.3 percent in 2016. The registration was also higher than it was in all previous elections going back to 2000.[28]

Voter participation in the 2020 election was 66.8 percent—just short of the 1992 record, according to the US Census Bureau, and Black Americans had a 63 percent participation, up from a 60 percent turnout in 2016. Hispanic turnout grew from 50 percent in 2008 to 54 percent in 2020. Comparatively, Hispanic turnout dropped during the Obama administration, falling to 48 percent in the 2012 and 2016 elections. Asian American voter participation increased by 10 percent in 2020 from 2016. Both Obama elections of 2008 and 2012 had a 47 percent Asian turnout.[29]

But 2020 could be controversial, so let's just talk about 2018—the least favorite year of Stacey Abrams, as she continues to claim without evidence that she was robbed. Presidential elections always have higher turnout than midterms, but 2018 nevertheless stood out. The overall voter turnout was 24 percent higher than in the previous midterm election of 2014, according to the US Census Bureau, which said it was one of the largest and most diverse turnouts in history.[30]

More than one hundred million ballots were cast in 2018, and Pew Research Center said, "All major racial and ethnic groups saw historic jumps in voter turnout" from the previous midterm election.[31] This included a 10.8 percent increase among Black voters and about 13 percent each for Hispanic and Asian voters.[32] In Georgia, by the way, Black voter turnout exceeded White voter turnout, according to the US Census Bureau. At 60 percent, Black turnout in the state in 2018 surpassed turnout in the 2016 election by 1 percent.[33]

Nevertheless, Abrams has continued in her cottage industries of writing books, establishing nonprofits, hitting the speaking circuit, and becoming a national power broker in the Democratic Party.

Aftermath of the Shelby County Decision

The voter suppression hysteria industrial complex frequently attacks the 2013 Supreme Court's *Shelby County v. Holder* ruling that very narrowly determined that Section 5 of the 1965 Voting Rights Act was outdated. Section 5 prevented states with a history of discrimination in voting from changing election laws without federal preclearance by the Justice Department. The section, when passed in 1965, was an emergency provision of the law that was supposed to last five years before coming up for renewal by Congress. It was subsequently renewed by Congress every five years. The covered states that had to get preclearance under Section 5 were Alabama, Alaska, Arizona, Georgia, Louisiana, Mississippi, South Carolina, Texas, and Virginia.

The VRA is in many ways a sacred law in fulfilling the promise of the Declaration of Independence and constitutional principles. It's easy to understand why someone from any political perspective might feel slicing away at even a small portion of the law runs the risk of turning back the clock.

But the fact is it didn't.

Shortly after the *Shelby County v. Holder* ruling in 2013, Attorney General Eric Holder said the Civil Rights Division of the Justice Department would "shift resources to the enforcement of Voting Rights Act provisions that were not affected by the Supreme Court's ruling—including Section 2, which prohibits voting discrimination based on race, color, or language—in addition to other federal voting rights laws."[34]

But during the Obama administration's two terms, the Justice Department filed five cases to enforce Section 2 of the Voting Rights Act. That's compared to the George W. Bush administration's Justice Department that filed sixteen cases over its two terms to enforce Section 2.

Why? Does it mean the Obama administration's DOJ wanted more racist voter suppression? No. It means there just weren't that many cases to prosecute.

The *Shelby County* decision was the justification in 2021 when the Democrat-controlled House pushed HR 4, dubbed the "John Lewis Voting Rights Advancement Act," a proposal to expand the 1965 Voting Rights Act to give the federal government veto power over state election laws, making Section 5 permanent for every state.

Again, this is using a rationale for Democrats to satisfy one of their prior goals of nationalizing machine politics when there is no factual basis behind the fear that any of the nine states covered by Section 5 cheated or that voter turnout was lower among Black voters. The only suppression that has emerged from the *Shelby County* decision is that facts are suppressing the hysteria projected by Democratic Party talking points.

The national turnout among the voting-eligible population in the 2012 election—the year before the *Shelby County* ruling—was 58 percent, according to the United States Elections Project. In the next presidential election, that rose nominally to 59.2 percent of eligible voters voting. In 2020, it rose to 67 percent.[35]

Of the nine states previously covered for preclearance under Section 5, the voter turnout either increased or remained the same in each. For example, Alabama (where the case originated) had a 58.6 percent turnout in 2012 and 58.8 percent in 2016. That rose to 63.1 percent in 2020. Georgia's voter participation was 59 percent in 2012 and 2016 but rose to 67 percent in 2020. From 2012 to 2020, Alaska rose from 52.6 percent to 68.8 percent. Louisiana went from 60.2 to 64.4 percent. Mississippi grew from 59.3 percent to 60.2 percent. South Carolina rose from 56.3 percent to 60.4 percent. Texas grew from 49.6 percent to 60.4 percent. Virginia saw a jump from 66.1 percent to 73 percent.[36]

Mississippi had a higher turnout percentage for each of those years than New York, Connecticut, and President Biden's home state of Delaware. In each of those elections, the percentage of Black Americans turning out to vote surpassed the percentage of white voters—not the case in the three blue states. Georgia likewise had an overall higher turnout than New York in 2016, 2018, and 2020. The Black turnout in Georgia for 2018 was 59.6 percent, and 64 percent in 2020. That's compared to 51.3 percent and 62.7 percent in New York for the same years.[37]

As Hans von Spakovsky, manager of the Election Law Reform Initiative at The Heritage Foundation and co-author of *Our Broken Elections*, told a Senate panel, "The claim that there is a wave of voter suppression going on across the country that requires expansion of the [Voting Rights Act] is simply false. Efforts to enhance the integrity of the election process through reforms such as voter identification requirements and improvements in the accuracy of statewide voter registration lists are not voter suppression."

If voter suppression was systemic, intuitively we would see fewer voters at each election, not more. If this was based on institutionalized racism, there would be fewer voters of color, not more.

Importantly, voter fraud is not systemic either, in that it permeates every election. But it is real and has had a demonstrable and proven effect on elections. To deny that is either being misinformed or lying.

Voter Fraud and Partisanship

One massive example of an organized voter fraud scam occurred when the nation was divided by the bloody Civil War. That's when Democrats tried to use mail-in voting to defeat Republican President Abraham Lincoln in 1864. Supporters of Democrat presidential nominee George McClellan used forged names and signatures on New York ballots. They brought in crates of fake ballots to New York, claiming these came from soldiers, even as some soldiers didn't know ballots were cast in their names. One of the conspirators said, "Dead or alive, they all had cast a good vote." A heroic poll checker named Oliver Wood foiled the fraud scheme. Law enforcement took voter fraud a little more seriously in those days, as leaders of the conspiracy to thwart democracy got life sentences. [38] Notably, Lincoln was comfortably re-elected and could have afforded to lose New York.

While there have been plenty of shady Republicans who have tried to steal elections, the bulk of culprits have been Democrats. University of Virginia political science professor Larry Sabato and then-*Wall Street Journal* reporter Glenn Simpson wrote in the 1996 book *Dirty Little Secrets* that Republican voters on average are wealthier than Democrat voters and the "pool of people who appear to be available and more vulnerable to an invitation to participate in vote fraud tend to lean Democratic," adding, "a poor person has more incentive to sell his vote than an upper-class suburbanite."[39] Moreover, a study of fraud by the Center for American Politics at the University of Maryland in 2004 determined most significant voter fraud cases "reportedly occur in inner cities," which are largely Democrat strongholds.[40]

Voter fraud has certainly been a bipartisan sport. The biggest proven voter fraud scandal in recent years—as will be detailed later—was a Republican congressional candidate who illegally won an election in North Carolina in 2018.

So, one would assume because of the mere fact that Republicans were involved in so much chicanery over the years that Democrats might care about laws to push honest elections as well. One would be wrong. Despite being on the wrong end of election fraud scandals themselves, Democrats are quick to dismiss the problem. The fact is that on balance, Democrats have probably benefited from fraud more.

In 2005, the report from the Commission on Federal Election Reform, better known as the Carter-Baker Commission (named for co-chairmen former Democratic President Jimmy Carter and former Republican Secretary of State James Baker), was greeted with much hoopla. Congress was unenthusiastic about doing anything other than providing lip service. But the partisan divide that had been subtle before began to grow wider after a bipartisan report.[41] Bipartisan support for the finding was there so long as it was limited to being another blue-ribbon commission of the government's finest minds submitting a report to set on a shelf and collect dust. Democrats perhaps didn't anticipate numerous state legislatures had the nerve to adopt some of the recommendations. When that happened, the Left took the de facto rebuttal to any proposal they don't like. They called it racist.

Age of the Machines

In 1789, Aaron Burr, before he became the nation's third and most sinister vice president, founded Tammany Hall. Lasting well into the early twentieth century, the machine did more than enough to honor the scoundrel's infamous legacy.

In what might make some Democrats proud today, Tammany worked to get prisoners released to ensure they voted and even established a "naturalization mill" to instantly turn immigrants coming off boats into voters. As the *Washington Post* explained, Tammany Hall bosses in New York "ushered hundreds of thousands on the Lower East Side and elsewhere into citizenship," to register to vote and keep Democrats in power. The *Post* continued: "The machine paid court fees and provided witnesses to testify that immigrants had been in the country the required five years. Sometimes, usually before crucial elections, immigrants were sworn in as citizens the day they arrived."[42]

Political machines like Tammany Hall with powerful party bosses thrived in part because they were the social service network at the time. The bosses helped arrange citizenship for immigrants, gave assistance for emergencies, and hooked people up with jobs— with the expectation these folks would pay back with voting. The machines didn't just trust them but used fraud and intimidation to ensure people made it to the polls.[43]

The most famous Tammany boss was William Marcy Tweed, who ran the machine in the late 1800s. He was good at what he did, but he eventually got caught and fessed up. During his testimony before the New York City Board of Alderman in 1877, Tweed said the operatives were directed to "count the ballots in bulk, or without counting them announce the result in bulk, or change from one to the other as the case may have been." He added, "The ballots made no results; the counter made the result. …That was generally done to every ward by the gentlemen who had charge of the ward."[44]

Other Tammany bosses who would do anything to get Democrats elected were kingpins John Kelly, Richard Croker, and Charles Francis Murphy.

There were many false starts to toppling the machine. The aforementioned New YorkGov. Samuel Tilden became an anti-establishment Democrat and took on Tammany Hall. It got him the Democratic presidential nomination in 1876. But Tammany outlived Tilden. In later years, Democratic Gov. William Sulzer fought Tammany but paid the price, getting impeached and removed from office in 1913.

Tammany's vice grip on New York politics couldn't last forever. Republican Mayor Fiorello Henry La Guardia and other reformers finally took down the machine during the Great Depression. Tammany lived into the 1960s but only as a shell of its past self before withering away.[45]

Machines managed to adapt to the changes in laws.

The Pendergast family of Kansas City, Missouri, started the machine in the late 1800s. James Pendergast was a saloon keeper and city alderman. He started the machine with his younger brother Tom Pendergast. Thousands of Pendergast cronies were on the Kansas City municipal payroll while doing nothing. The Pendergast machine also had national influence and backed Franklin D. Roosevelt—a Democrat opponent of Tammany—at the 1932 Democratic National Convention. Pendergast cronies were rewarded with key federal government jobs under the New Deal. Even more important than backing FDR, the Pendergast machine was behind the budding political career of young Harry Truman by first getting him elected as a state judge.[46]

Mayor Frank Hague ran Jersey City, New Jersey, from 1917 to 1947 and somehow amassed a fortune of $10 million from an $8,000 annual salary. He was a crafty machine boss, head of the state's Democratic Party, and often decided who the next governor and members of New Jersey's congressional delegation would be from his Jersey City perch.[47]

When the Honest Ballot Association sent Princeton students to be poll watchers, they were brutalized for their efforts. The election superintendent griped his deputies were intimidated and that, "The only way to have an honest election in Hudson County under the present conditions is with the militia."[48]

Later, the Daley machine emerged. The six-term Chicago Mayor Richard Daley's organization wielded significant national influence, statewide influence, and essentially controlled local politics. As the *Chicago Tribune* said, "Once an election has been stolen in Cook County, it stays stolen."[49]

During its highest point, the Daley machine controlled ten congressional seats, the Democrat caucus in the state legislature, and the governor—along with Cook County and Chicago. The Daley machine doled out free turkeys, free booze, and government jobs, but only to those loyal in turning out the vote to keep the machine in power. If there weren't enough votes, Daley's operation would find them.[50]

John F. Kennedy won Illinois by nine thousand votes. At one point, it appeared that Nixon would carry Illinois. Daley held back the Chicago vote until late on election night and then released it for a massive Kennedy win in Cook County by 450,000 votes.[51] The 1960 presidential election resulted in massive irregularities in Chicago and Texas. Both states were extremely close. The *Tribune* later reported "gross and palpable fraud" throughout

Chicago. It's not clear if the election would have flipped the other way without fraud, but it has remained a long-running mystery.

Democrats have been MVPs at machine-driven voter fraud since Burr's grand creation, but the party hasn't been the only culprits. They are just better at building the infrastructure to make it work.

In recent decades, laws have evolved to make it difficult to cheat the system, with more checks and balances on ballot handling and counting, voting machines that are tested and certified and not connected to a central network to prevent hacking. Also, election workers are better trained than in the machine era. More safeguards are in place. But it's far from perfect, and voter fraud IS STILL a problem. This is demonstrated by legal findings, overturned elections, people jailed, and criminal charges.[52]

It was the machines that resisted these changes to keep elections more honest. Today the spirit of the machines lives on through Democrats in Congress cranking out legislation such as HR 1, along with various nonprofits battling against voter ID and other proposals.

Voter Fraud Deniers

When the Supreme Court upheld the Indiana voter ID law in 2008 by a 6–3 vote, liberal Justice John Paul Stevens wrote in the majority opinion in *Crawford v. Marion County Election Board*, "It remains true, however, that flagrant examples of such fraud…have been documented throughout this Nation's history by respected historians and journalists, that occasional examples have surfaced in recent years…[and] that not only is the risk of voter fraud real but it could affect the outcome of a close election."[53]

A grand jury report on a massive voter fraud scam from the 1997 Miami mayor's race laid out the larger stakes of fighting fraud. "The right to vote defines the essence of American citizenship. It provides the bedrock upon which our democratic form of government survives," the grand jury report says. "The greatest social struggles in our history, from the emotional impetus for the American Revolution itself, to the struggle for women's suffrage and the battle for civil rights, have all had at their core the acquisition of the vote for those who were disenfranchised. To a democracy, there can be no greater crime than voter fraud. A single falsely cast vote corrupts the entire electoral process."[54]

Voter fraud deniers frequently point to the lack of convictions for voter fraud as evidence it doesn't exist. Secondly, they argue, that if it does exist at all, it's not enough to make a difference in the outcome. Third, they insist voter fraud in America never happens at a large-scale or coordinated level. All are inaccurate and are straw man arguments.

No, there is absolutely no cabal determining the large swath of all election outcomes. Election fraud isn't rampant and systemic. Your vote still matters. What's demonstrably true is that well after the demise of the corrupt political machines, such as Tammany Hall, fraud has continued as a grand tradition in American democracy—leading to prosecutions and to legal findings that overturned or voided an election outcome.

Frequently cited by the deniers is a 2007 analysis from the Brennan Center for Justice that claims voter fraud incident rates are between 0.0003 and 0.025 percent between 2000 and 2004. Such an estimate is ridiculously low but largely misses the point either way.[55]

As the Carter-Baker Commission correctly says, the threat "is not the magnitude of voter fraud" to be concerned about. Rather, "In close or disputed elections, and there are many, a small amount of fraud could make the margin of difference."

You will see a lot about the Brennan Center for Justice in these pages, as it has been one of the most prominent and long-standing organizations behind the voter suppression hysteria industrial complex and a key element of the modern machine. The nonprofit is part of the New York University School of Law, named for liberal Supreme Court Justice William J. Brennan. The center was established in 1995 after Brennan's former clerks raised $5 million to establish it. The center functions as a mix between an activist organization and a think tank, as it tracks legislation, lobbies, drafts legislation, and engages in legal action.[56] You will also see plenty on the more recently established Fair Fight Action, which Stacey Abrams founded to tout the voter suppression line.

The Brennan Center for Justice has been involved in numerous left-wing causes but became largely consumed in voter fraud denial in 2006, issuing a report, "Citizens Without Proof," claiming that voter ID laws would disenfranchise millions of minorities, poor, and elderly voters who are deemed less likely to have a photo ID.[57] The report was issued the year after the Carter-Baker Commission report called for voter ID across the nation. These dire predictions, like others that would follow, didn't come true.

Voiding Fraudulent Elections

Many Democrats and Republicans will go to their graves believing certain elections were stolen. In some cases, they may be correct, but it's not always provable. There are, however, numerous cases of adjudicated election fraud that flipped the election outcomes.

The Heritage Foundation's Election Fraud database, which is only a sampling of cases, shows at least 1,365 legally proven instances of voter fraud since 1982.[58] Elections overturned by fraud are generally at the local level. But it's the local level that is closest to the people. Since 1992, at least twenty-seven election results were voided, overturned, or the winner was ordered to vacate office after judicial findings or election officials found provable voter fraud.[59, 60]

Here are just a few examples of elections voided after fraud:

- In May 2022, a California judge overturned a Compton City Council election. In a 2021 runoff election for a council seat, Isaac Galvan defeated Andre Spicer by one vote. However, five people were subsequently charged with conspiracy to commit election fraud and pleaded guilty. The judge tossed four votes cast by people that lived outside the city and declared Spicer the official winner. [61]

- In 2019, Brian Hodge was convicted on federal charges in a vote-buying conspiracy to get Republican Randy White elected as sheriff of Monroe County, Tennessee. White won by seven hundred votes defeating incumbent Democratic Sheriff Bill Bivens. However, White was removed from office amid the scandal.[62]

- In a 2018 Texas case, Armando O'Caña seemingly won a run-off race for mayor in Mission, Texas, beating incumbent Norberto "Beto" Salinas. But after strong evidence emerged that the O'Caña campaign had bribed voters, tampered with absentee ballots, and improperly "assisted" voters at the polls, state Judge J. Bonner Dorsey invalidated the result.[63]

- In 2016, Missouri state Rep. Penny Hubbard won the Democratic primary in the state's 78th House District by just ninety votes. Her opponent, Bruce Franks Jr., contested the outcome over a lopsided absentee vote tally. State Judge Rex Burlison ruled that enough improper absentee ballots were cast to change the results and ordered a new election. Franks won by 1,533 votes.[64]

- After a 2012 federal investigation of a voter fraud conspiracy in West Virginia, Lincoln County Sheriff Jerry Bowman and County Clerk Donald Whitten pleaded guilty to stuffing ballot boxes and falsifying absentee ballots to try to steal a Democratic primary election in 2010. Lincoln County Commissioner Thomas Ramey pleaded guilty to lying to investigators. Bowman and Ramey were involved in helping Whitten get re-elected. He won the primary, but a judge overturned the election, tossing out three hundred fraudulent ballots.[65]

- In 2006, the Tennessee State Senate voided the election of Democrat Ophelia Ford—who is part of the state's Ford political dynasty. This came after revelations that three poll workers in Memphis faked votes on machines to help her get elected. They cast at least two in the names of dead people.[66]

Large-Scale Scams

In a Brennan Center for Justice paper, President Biden's future voting czar, Justin Levitt, has given the Left a reference point to say voter fraud isn't real. The argument is that to the extent voter fraud exists at all, that it's just some lone yahoo and never a grand conspiracy. What the Brennan Center calls its seminal report says: "Allegations of widespread fraud by malevolent voters are easy to make, but often prove to be inaccurate. The Brennan Center has analyzed public materials in some of the areas branded as notorious election fraud 'hot spots,' finding that various election irregularities led to inflated claims of widespread fraud." The report argues, "Overly restrictive identification requirements for voters at the polls—which address a sort of voter fraud more rare than death by lightning—is only the most prominent example."[67]

A reading of Levitt's 2007 report titled, "The Truth About Voter Fraud," actually reveals a good bit of hedging in making the argument that this is nothing to worry about.

It often has been a single yahoo. But there have been significant cases of either campaign officials or local government officials attempting to rig elections.

Conspiracy cases that have been charged and investigated include:

- In June 2022, a federal investigation of an old-fashioned ballot box stuffing scandal in Philadelphia wrapped up with the conviction of the ringleader, former Democrat Congressman Michael "Ozzie" Myers. [68] The probe of elections spanning from 2014 through 2019 began under the Trump administration's Justice Department and had continued charging individuals under the Biden Justice Department. Myers pleaded guilty months after a federal grand jury indicted him and charged smaller players who were polling place workers who were party of the Myers operation. Federal prosecutors said the election workers aligned with Myers were casting multiple votes in voting machines and encouraged legal voters to cast fraudulent votes. The ballot box stuffing was aimed largely at local judicial races that can be decided by a dozen votes, explained Patrick Christmas, policy director for the Committee of Seventy, a group founded in 1904 to oppose corruption in Philadelphia. The indictments refer to fraud in "federal, state, and local elective offices," which was enough to make it a federal case. [69] Philadelphia City Commissioner Al Schmidt, a Republican, who is one of three officials responsible for elections and voter registration, spotted the matter and reported first in a referral to the Justice Department in 2014. [70]

- Texas Attorney General Ken Paxton charged four people—including a county commissioner—with a total of 134 felony charges for voter fraud from the 2018 Democratic primary. The group allegedly wanted young able-bodied voters to vote fraudulently by mail, claiming they were disabled. [71]

- In the city of East St. Louis, Illinois, a group of precinct committeemen—Charles Powell, Sheila Thomas, Jesse

Lewis, and Kelvin Ellis, along with precinct worker Yvette Johnson, were convicted of conspiracy to commit election fraud. They paid for votes in the 2004 election. They even used city funds to pay voters to support Democrat candidates.[72]

- In 1984, a Brooklyn grand jury determined that eight Democratic primary elections from 1968 to 1982 were tainted by excessive fraud that it called Tammany Hall-like tactics. The grand jury report says, "The ease and boldness with which these fraudulent schemes were carried out shows the vulnerability of our entire electoral process to unscrupulous and fraudulent manipulation," the report said. It continued, "Methods must be devised to secure the integrity of elections." Brooklyn District Attorney Elizabeth Holtzman said at the time that it was "imperative" the Brooklyn office of the Board of Elections adopt new procedures "so that serious fraud does not occur in voting this fall." The grand jury's investigation was prompted by the case of former New York state Sen. Vander L. Beatty, convicted of forgery and conspiracy in a vast voter registration scheme in which his supporters forged hundreds of registration cards to the Brooklyn office of the Board of Elections in 1982 when forgeries were used as part of an unsuccessful post-election challenge.[73]

- And there is of course, Chicago—a punchline for political corruption. A Justice Department investigation determined that one hundred thousand fraudulent ballots were cast in the 1982 election. This resulted in convictions for sixty-three fraudsters for charges of vote buying, voting under someone else's name, phony voter registration, voting from noncitizens, and phony absentee ballots.[74]

Given this history, even recent history, it's little wonder why states would consistently upgrade election laws. As has been the case since the 1800s, the machine—or the modern day equivalent—has always gone into hyperdrive to oppose reform. The tool of choice has been to just lie.

Chapter 2

Lies and Truth about State Election Reforms

Confronting the shoddy history of voter denial in the United States is important because—as with anything else in history—we are not doomed to repeat it. That doesn't mean demagoguing every reform as a return to the past.

The Left needed a sob story to provide a smidgen of evidence to their myth of nefarious and rampant voter suppression in 2021. So, Priorities USA—a Democrat super PAC—provided one. The party of the downtrodden's choice for a victim was a Yale graduate student.

The challenge was against limits on ballot harvesting in the 2021 Florida voting law and why the student couldn't just mail a ballot himself instead of handing it off to a ballot collector. Asked in a deposition why returning a ballot to Florida was an undue burden, he explained the nearest post office was thirty minutes from his home. When asked if he ever Googled a post office closer to his home, he answered in the negative. It turned out the Yale student wasn't aware he could use the mailbox at his apartment and that there were also public mailboxes six blocks away from his apartment.

Shortly after the debacle of a deposition, Priorities USA dropped the case.

Left-leaning organizations challenging election integrity laws in Arizona, Florida, Iowa, Maine, Michigan, New Hampshire, Ohio, South Carolina, and Wisconsin also fared poorly, wrote Kyle Hupfer, general counsel for the Republican National Committee—whose legal team routinely squares off against the Democratic National Committee in court over state election laws.[75]

Courts—for the most part—aren't buying the hysteria about state laws. Meanwhile, Democrats' attempt to enact legislation that would restore the days of Tammany Hall and take it national seemed all but thwarted by early 2022 after two Democrats in battleground seats refused the push by leadership, the progressive wing, and finally President Joe Biden to kill the filibuster.

The war will continue to be waged over how elections will be fought. But a new form of the old political machine senses the opportunity for a comeback at a national level that would put Tammany Hall, the Daley machine, and others to shame. The only bulwark appears to be state laws that, when honestly looked at, do not prevent any eligible voters from casting a ballot.

The machine comeback is in the form of federal legislation to wipe away state election integrity laws.

President Biden traveled to Atlanta in January 2022 to attack the voting laws.

"Last year alone, 19 states not proposed but enacted 34 laws attacking voting rights. There were nearly 400 additional bills Republican members of state legislatures tried to pass and now, Republican legislators in several states have already announced plans to escalate the onslaught this year," the president said. "Their endgame? To turn the will of the voters into a mere suggestion—something states can respect or ignore. Jim Crow 2.0 is about two insidious things: voter suppression and election subversion. It's no longer about who gets to vote; it's about making it harder to vote. It's about who gets to count the vote and whether your vote counts at all. It's not hyperbole; this is a fact."[76]

It's neither hyperbole nor fact. It's demonstrably false.

In March 2022, during his first State of the Union, Biden lied again about the state election laws.

"The most fundamental right in America is the right to vote and have it counted, and look, it's under assault," Biden said. "In state after state, new laws have been passed not only to suppress the vote—we've been there before—but to subvert the entire election. We can't let this happen."

When most public opinion polling showed support for state election reforms, the left-wing machine's de facto position was to lie about the laws. Supporters of Tammany Hall 2.0 tactics—which we explore in later chapters—told us these laws were Jim Crow 2.0, that voter ID would make it difficult for the poor and minorities to vote, that the laws banned ballot drop boxes, and that water was being banned in voting lines—all of which we explain below is false.

In 2021, at least nineteen states passed major election reforms, according to the National Conference of State Legislatures. The bills broadly required voter ID, curbing the controversial practice of ballot harvesting, and removing dead and other ineligible voters from registration rolls.

Many of the bills were large and sweeping. Four states got the most attention—or were most targeted for ridicule—for these laws: Arizona, Florida, Georgia, and Texas. Lying about these state laws was a necessary pretext for Tammany Hall 2.0 to pass the national election takeover bills that would erase most safeguards. So here's a fact check of the biggest lies about the election laws. First, maybe the biggest and definitely most brazen lie is not specific to one state.

Lie: The new state election laws and future state laws just around the corner will allow Republicans to set aside election results at will and install their candidate, voters be damned. Your votes won't count. What's even worse, it's all part of a coup to get Donald Trump elected again in 2024.

Truth: It seems Democrats and other media outlets mainstreamed this scary notion after a particularly irresponsible piece of journalism in *The Atlantic* by Barton Gellman, with the headline "Trump's Next Coup Has Already Begun," published in December 2021.[77] Everything scary has to tie back to Trump, right? Add the word "coup," and it's great clickbait.

The left-wing *Mother Jones* ran a piece titled, "The Coming Coup: How Republicans Are Laying the Groundwork to Steal Future Elections," which bashed the voting laws in Georgia and other states, while claiming Republicans would win majorities through gerrymandering to further wreck democracy in hopes of reinstalling Trump in 2024.[78]

Even the Associated Press had a piece with a scary partisan headline about a "Slow-Motion Insurrection" resulting from Republican state election laws.[79]

Other outlets simply cited *The Atlantic*, which specifically targeted Georgia and Arizona laws but warned other GOP legislatures would adopt laws supposedly allowing the at-will overturning of elections to nullify voting—all of which is rather absurd.

The new Georgia law did give the state legislature more control to replace members of the state election board and county election boards. It also diminished the role of the secretary of state—an elected official in partisan races.[80]

None of that means it's going to be a board stacked with partisans. "The secretary of state will no longer chair the State Election Board, becoming instead a non-voting ex-officio member," Georgia Public Broadcasting explained. "The new chair would be nonpartisan but appointed by a majority of the state House and Senate. …The chair would not be allowed to have been a candidate, participate in a political party organization or campaign or [have] made campaign contributions for two years prior to being appointed."[81]

As for taking over local election boards, this is largely a problem that has been long in the making in Georgia. Fulton

County, the state's largest voting jurisdiction, was controversial for years because of its inefficient and poorly managed elections. During the Georgia Democratic primary in 2020, Fulton County voters had to stand in line for hours. A state-appointed independent monitor reported sloppy practices and poor management, however, saw no evidence of "any dishonesty, fraud or intentional malfeasance."[82] Nevertheless, sloppy can lead to disenfranchising voters or votes not getting properly counted.

The 2020 election—for better or worse—was what prompted lawmakers to finally act. The new Georgia provision aims to stop nepotism, incompetence, and patronage for members of election boards. The Georgia law will allow a bipartisan State Election Board to do performance reviews of local election supervisors that consistently have problems, such as long lines and not fulfilling absentee ballot requests. But the law requires an evidentiary hearing for removal for problems with two elections in a row.

Above all else, the state board of elections has NO power to overturn election results.

The Atlantic piece also blasts the Arizona legislature for passing a law that prevents the Democrat Secretary of State Katie Hobbs from taking part in election lawsuits, leaving it instead with the state attorney general. Again, massive omissions here, meaning the writer was woefully uninformed or just vested in his narrative. Viewing this as a crisis fails to realize first that Hobbs is a candidate for governor, which Georgia Democrats argued was a conflict when Secretary of State Brian Kemp ran for governor there. More importantly, Hobbs's Democrat predecessor, Michele Reagan, had entered a consent decree with the liberal League of United Latin American Citizens, or LULAC, in 2018, agreeing to allow voter registration without proof of citizenship requirements. That November, before the consent decree was in effect, 1,700 individuals voted without providing proof of citizenship. In the 2020 election, the first election operating under the consent decree, 11,600 voted without documentary proof of citizenship.

So, it's easy to see why a legislature wouldn't want a secretary of state entering more consent decrees favorable to Democrats when election lawsuits emerge.[83]

Regarding future presidential races, *The Atlantic* went on to say: "Republicans are promoting an 'independent state legislature doctrine, which holds that statehouses have 'plenary,' or exclusive, control of the rules for choosing presidential electors. Taken to its logical conclusion, it could provide a legal basis for any state legislature to throw out an election result it dislikes and appoint its preferred electors instead."

What might shock Gellman is that something called the Constitution empowers state legislators with appointing electors on behalf of their states in any way they choose. In the first contested presidential election of 1796, only seven of the sixteen states had popular voting. That began to expand under Jacksonian democracy, and state legislatures passed laws affirming the popular vote would decide which slate of electors were sent to the Electoral College. Over time, as a matter of efficiency, most state legislatures delegated the procedural powers of certifying electors to the governor, secretary of state, or another chief state election official. It's along the same lines that states decide how to apportion electors now, as forty-eight states have a winner-take-all system, while two states—Maine and Nebraska—award electors based on congressional districts. The Constitution doesn't require electors to go along with the popular will of their state's voters, but thirty-two states and the District of Columbia have laws that impose fines and penalties for "faithless electors" that opt to vote for someone else. The Supreme Court upheld the right of state legislatures to pass such laws.[84]

To be clear, state legislatures have always been able to claw back the authority to appoint presidential electors and tell their own voters tough luck. But to claim such is patently silly because all state legislators are elected.

Yes, there have been bills proposed in state legislatures that would in some cases radically expand the state legislature's power to award electors. *The Atlantic* piece, referencing a dubious left-wing pressure group, said Republicans are pushing this in fifteen state legislatures. But such legislation hasn't passed. And guess what? It won't. State lawmakers want to get reelected, and party leaders want to hold onto majorities. One way to tick off voters is to seize their power to vote for president.

The only legislatures that have passed laws to ignore the will of their state's voters have been those voting to join the National Popular Vote Interstate Compact, committing to award their electors to whatever candidate carries the popular vote regardless of the votes of their state residents. The compact will not take effect until enough states with 270 electoral votes join. Importantly, virtually every state in the compact that prioritizes the national vote over their state residents has been blue.

Lie: Voter suppression is systemic in American elections and Republicans are committing it with impunity.

Truth: Here again, there is not a law on the books regarding "voter suppression," but vote denial, voter intimidation, and vote dilution are illegal. To be clear, there have been bad actors from both parties—sometimes in a concerted or conspiratorial manner—that have engaged in the illegal activity of vote denial, voter intimidation, or vote dilution. In most cases, this led to consequences.

Here are some examples:

- In the 1980s, the Republican National Committee hired off-duty police officers to monitor certain polling places in New Jersey and Louisiana. Both states have longstanding reputations for political corruption and voter fraud. The problem is that the off-duty cops were sent primarily to minority areas of these states. [85] Democrats sued, alleging voter intimidation, and the RNC signed a 1982 consent decree to forgo any "ballot security" measures. This restraint endured for thirty-eight years before Republicans could resume even nominal ballot security in 2020. [86]

- In 2006, four employees of the John Kerry 2004 presidential campaign were convicted for slashing the tires of 25 vans that the Wisconsin Republican Party rented to drive GOP election monitors and voters to polling places. Milwaukee County Court Judge Michael B. Brennan sentenced the four Democrats to four-to-six months in jail, telling the defendants: "Voter suppression has no place in our country. Your crime took away that right to vote for some citizens."[87]

- On Election Day in 2008, members of the New Black Panther Party stood outside a polling place in Philadelphia wearing paramilitary attire shouting racial comments at White voters. After a viral YouTube video that appeared to be voter intimidation, the Justice Department under the Bush administration started an investigation and filed a civil suit under the Voting Rights Act. But the Obama administration dropped the lawsuit shortly after taking office.[88]

- In 2011, Paul Schurick was convicted on charges of fraud and conspiracy. Schurick was the campaign manager for former Republican Maryland Gov. Bob Ehrlich, who ran in 2010 to try to reclaim his old job. Schurick authorized robocalls that went to 112,000 voters in mostly minority areas that pretended to be a Democrat telling voters before Election Day to "relax" because Democratic Gov. Martin O'Malley had already won. [89]

These are the notably adjudicated cases of attempting to prevent eligible voters from exercising their right to vote. However, it's a tough sell to claim any of these changed the result of an election. The RNC paid a heavy price for its shenanigans and ceded ground nationally to Democrats in state-level get-out-the-vote efforts and election challenges for almost four decades. Wisconsin was close in 2004 between Kerry and President George W. Bush, but it's unlikely the tire-slashing put Kerry over the top. Barack Obama handily carried Pennsylvania in 2008 and didn't need any panther help. O'Malley was re-elected governor in 2010.

Lie: Each state that passed the Republican-led legislation will lead to mass voter suppression in the state.

Truth: As noted earlier, Democrats' warning that voter ID laws would suppress turnout never came true. Yes, it's still early to comprehensively judge every law. But the two most controversial laws have been in Georgia and Texas. Both states have had voting that we can compare to previous years.

In Georgia, turnout for early voting hit record highs for the state's 2022 primary election, surging by about four times what it was in the comparable year of 2018, also a midterm election primary.[90]

In Texas, where Democrats left the state to live the high life in Washington, DC, as political theater, the voter turnout was also higher. The 2022 primary saw 3.03 million voters turn out to vote in races for governor, statewide offices, and congressional seats. In the comparable 2018 primary where voters chose nominees for both a governor's race and a US Senate race, the turnout was 2.59 million.

"This just shows the people are actually seeing through a lot of this garbage that's coming from the Democrats. And it's really good to see that we're having strong turnout," Rep. Claudia Tenney, R-NY, the co-chair of the House Election Integrity Caucus, told me in an interview. "The people are actually going to take back the government from these authoritarians, from these huge government bureaucracies that the Democrats are trying to create and take over by undermining our election laws."

If Georgia and Texas were supposed to be the worst of the worst, the turnout numbers alone expose the Big Lie about the 2021 election reform laws. It's still worth taking a state-by-state look at the lies and truth about the four highest-profile election reform bills. While nineteen states enacted election integrity legislation, some had more depth than others, while others came under more attack by Democrats and the media than others. But most states adopted measures similar to those of Arizona, Florida, Georgia, and Texas.

Arizona

While the other states passed election omnibus bills, the Arizona legislature passed and Gov. Doug Ducey signed a series of separate election reform bills. One of the new laws requires the secretary of state to compare death records with a statewide voter registration database. Another law enhances the security of voting machines. The Grand Canyon State also banned private money from paying for election administration—a response to Mark Zuckerberg's money pouring in.

One new Arizona law removed the names of inactive voters from an early-voting list if they had not voted in two consecutive election cycles. And another law requires voters to sign the envelope in which they submit an absentee ballot.

Here's a look at the Left's lies.

Lie: Arizona is purging voters from voter registration lists.

Truth: SB 1485 says that individuals who have not voted in four consecutive primary and general elections will get a notice in the mail giving them the opportunity to stay on the state's early voting list. If these folks don't respond, they can still be added back to the early voting list at any time and can still vote early in person or in person on election day. Another law, HB2054, was designed to remove dead people's names from the voter registration rolls. The deceased probably won't mind having their names removed, even if Democrats mind.

Lie: Arizona voter ID requirements for Arizona's mail-in voting make it tough to vote.

Truth: These are the same voter ID requirements for absentee voting that did not harm voter turnout for in-person voting among any demographics. This would just require filling in a driver's license number or another government-issued ID number.

Florida

A Florida law signed by Gov. Ron DeSantis restricts ballot harvesting and bans private funding of election administration. The law requires voters to request an absentee ballot to receive one. It also increases security for ballot drop boxes, which made their debut in the 2020 election because of the COVID-19 pandemic.

Lie: Florida's law makes it tougher for seniors and disabled voters to get absentee ballots turned in by others.

Truth: There is no shortage of seniors in Florida, so Democrats resorted to this line of attack when defending their ballot harvesting tactics, which have been a valuable asset to the Democrat machine. But ballot harvesting has been an embarrassing part of the state's legacy. At long last, the 2021 reform allows someone to collect absentee ballots from immediate family members but no more than two ballots from non-family members. This means no political operatives trolling nursing homes and rounding up ballots. The provision not only prevents voter intimidation but better secures a chain of custody for the ballot.

Lie: The Florida law's ID requirements suppress voting.

Truth: The Florida law strengthened voter ID requirements for absentee voting by making them uniform with in-person voting. The law required ID—in the form of a driver's license number or another ID number—for mail-in ballot requests.[91]

Lie: The Florida law limits drop boxes to suppress voting.

Truth: Ballot drop boxes were not widely used before COVID-19 and were an emergency action in 2020 to attempt to make voting seem safer for an understandably squeamish country that wanted to avoid crowded voting areas. There's really no need to bring them back. But the Florida law does. Only this time around, staffing and monitoring of drop boxes will ensure ballots are safe. The law requires drop box locations to be published a month in advance so voters will know where to go.

Georgia

The Georgia law has been the most maligned by politicians and woke corporations caving to far-left pressure.

The law establishes guidelines for ballot drop boxes, aims to shorten lines at polling places, and as mentioned, gives a state election board more oversight over county election administration. The measure also prohibits political operatives from offering food, bottled water, or anything of value within 150 feet of polls. Only New York and Montana have similar provisions related to offering food and water in voting lines.

Big tech firms such as Facebook and Google jumped onto the absurd narrative—not shocking since so many states have banned billionaires from bankrolling election administration.

"We support making voting as accessible and broad-based as possible and oppose efforts to make it harder for people to vote," Facebook says.[92]

There were endless lies and mischaracterizations of the bill. Here are just a few.

Lie: The law bans drinking water while waiting in line. Biden said: "It makes it a crime to provide water to voters while they wait in line—lines Republican officials themselves have created by reducing the number of polling sites across the state, disproportionately in Black neighborhoods."

Truth: The law allows official poll workers, as opposed to campaign workers, to provide water to voters. Specifically, the law says: "No person shall solicit votes in any manner or by any means or method, nor shall any person distribute or display any campaign material, nor shall any person give, offer to give, or participate in the giving of any money or gifts, including, but not limited to, food and drink, to an elector, nor shall any person solicit signatures for any petition, nor shall any person, other than election officials discharging their duties, establish or set up any tables or booths on any day in which ballots are being cast: (1) Within 150 feet of the outer edge of any building within which a polling place is established; (2) Within any polling place; or (3) Within 25 feet of any voter standing in line to vote at any polling place."

The law goes on to state: "This Code section shall not be construed to prohibit a poll officer from distributing materials, as required by law, which are necessary for the purpose of instructing electors or from distributing materials prepared by the Secretary of State which are designed solely for the purpose of encouraging voter participation in the election being conducted or from making available self-service water from an unattended receptacle to an elector waiting in line to vote."

Further, Biden's claim that Republicans "created" the long lines ignores the longstanding ineptitude of the heavily Democrat-leaning Fulton County. Entirely separate from the water lie, Senate Bill 202 requires large precincts that have had lines that stretch for more than one hour to add personnel and more voting machines for the next election.[93]

Lie: The Georgia voter ID requirement is way too onerous. Biden said, "It adds rigid restrictions on casting absentee ballots that will effectively deny the right to vote to countless voters."

Truth: The Georgia law requires a driver's license number or a free state ID number to cast an absentee ballot. Since 97 percent of Georgians have one of those, it's difficult to see how this would be onerous. The ID number replaced signature verification, which could be difficult and subjective. A voter can also put the last four digits of their Social Security number on the ballot application form.[94, 95]

The law states: "If the elector does not have a Georgia driver's license or state identification card issued pursuant to Article 5 of Chapter 5 of Title 40, the elector shall so affirm in the space provided on the outer oath envelope and print the last four digits of his or her Social Security number in the space provided on the outer oath envelope."

Lie: The law reduces the number of days to vote.

Truth: The total number of early voting days remains the same under the 2021 law, while the weekend voting gets a boost. No-excuse absentee voting continues. To be fair to critics, under the 2021 law, the earliest that Georgia voters may request an application for an absentee ballot will be seventy-seven days before Election Day, down from the previous 180 days.[96]

Lie: The law bans ballot drop boxes. The *New York Times* even referred to the legislation as a "GOP-backed bill that prohibits the use of drop boxes."[97]

Truth: The law codifies ballot drop boxes. But for SB 202, the emergency measure would not have to be used in any future Georgia elections. That said, fewer drop boxes will be available in future elections—presumably operating in the absence of a pandemic—than in the 2020 election. Each of the 159 counties in Georgia must provide at least one drop box. But boxes will have to be located near early-voting sites and be accessible for dropping off absentee ballots when these polling locations are open.

Lie: Biden said, "Among the outrageous parts of this new state law, it ends voting hours early so working people can't cast their vote after their shift is over."

Truth: The new Georgia law does nothing to change Election Day voting hours from 7 a.m. to 7 p.m., although it expands weekend voting before Election Day. Georgia Public Broadcasting, the state affiliate of the left-leaning Public Broadcasting Service (which includes National Public Radio), did an explanatory piece that said: "One of the biggest changes in the bill would expand early voting access for most counties, adding an additional mandatory Saturday and formally codifying Sunday voting hours as optional."[98]

The law itself states: "Requiring two Saturday voting days and two optional Sunday voting days will dramatically increase the total voting hours for voters across the State of Georgia, and all electors in Georgia will have access to multiple opportunities to vote in person on the weekend for the first time."

The Georgia Public Broadcasting story also says: "Counties can have early voting open as long as 7 a.m. to 7 p.m., or 9 a.m. to 5 p.m. at minimum."[99]

The legislation signed into law by Kemp does limit the time for runoff campaigns from nine weeks after Election Day to four weeks. But it says early voting in these runoff elections should begin "as soon as possible prior to a runoff from any other general primary."

The law reads: "Voting shall be conducted during normal business hours beginning at 9:00 A.M. and ending at 5:00 P.M. on weekdays, other than observed state holidays, during such period and shall be conducted on the second Saturday and third Saturdays during the hours of 9:00 A.M. through 5:00 P.M. and, if the registrar or absentee ballot clerk so chooses, the second Sunday, the third Sunday, or both the second and third Sundays prior to a primary or election during the hours of 9:00 A.M. through 4:00 P.M. determined by the registrar or absentee ballot clerk, but no longer than 7:00 A.M. through 7:00 P.M."

Lie: Voters going to the wrong precinct are banned from voting.

Truth: If a voter shows up at the wrong precinct, local election officials are directed to tell voters to travel to their correct precinct to cast a vote. However, the Georgia law has an exception for voters who show up at the wrong precinct after 5 p.m. on Election Day. Because polls close at 7 p.m., the election officials will accept a provisional ballot from the voter who arrived at the wrong location within two hours of the polls closing. According to the National Conference of State Legislatures, that's better than half the states—including some of the most heavily Democrat states. States that don't count provisional ballots if cast at the wrong precinct are Connecticut, Biden's home state of Delaware, Hawaii, Illinois, Michigan, Nevada, Vermont, Virginia, and Wisconsin.

Texas

The new Texas law extends early voting hours, prohibits election clerks from mailing out an application for an absentee ballot unless a voter requests one, and bans "drive-through" voting. The measure also requires voter ID for mail-in ballots and safeguards for citizen poll watchers.

Texas state Rep. Michelle Beckley, among the Democrat lawmakers that fled Texas to avoid voting for the election reform bill, said the law makes "it harder to vote by mail."[100]

This wasn't the biggest lie.

Lie: The Texas law suppresses voting by banning drive-through and outdoor voting.

Truth: Drive-through voting was a pandemic phenomenon. It also wasn't done across the state. It was predominantly in Harris County, or the Houston area, which has one of the most problematic histories with sloppy election administration and proven election fraud. With vaccines widely available, future elections won't need drive-through voting.

Lie: That law allows Republicans to intimidate voters and election officials. Biden said, "In Texas, for example, the Republican-led state legislature wants to allow partisan poll watchers to intimidate voters and imperil impartial poll workers."

Truth: The Texas law gives more autonomy to partisan poll watchers, granting them "free movement" at polling places as long as it's not in the voting booth when a voter casts a ballot. The legislation would make it a crime for an election worker in Texas to obstruct the view of a poll watcher or position him or her "in a manner that would make observation not reasonably effective."[101] The previous Texas law allowed poll watchers to sit or stand "conveniently near" election workers.

Let's also be clear. A bully can't show up at a polling place and declare himself or herself an election observer. A person must be pre-certified and legally approved. Generally, Democrats and Republicans show up to check voting and the other side.[102]

In the 2020 election, there were several verified cases across the country of local election officials having the poll watchers illegally removed from a polling site. Other poll watchers were obstructed from observing the process.[103]

It has long been accepted that election observers play an important role in free and fair elections. The 2005 Carter-Baker Commission report says, "All legitimate domestic and international election observers should be granted unrestricted access to the election process, provided that they accept election rules, do not interfere with the electoral process, and respect the secrecy of the ballot."

The State Department sends election observers to budding democracies around the world. The 1965 Voting Rights Act has an entire section authorizing federal observers.[104]

Lie: Texas is limiting mail-in and early voting.

Truth: The law adds a voter ID requirement to absentee voting. Much like Georgia, the Texas law allows more early voting than many blue states. Texas allows two weeks of early in-person voting. Further, the law allowed for voting access between 6 a.m. and 9 p.m., which is longer than blue states such as Maryland and New Mexico. The Texas law also allows voters to track their applications and absentee ballot online, determining when it will come to their home and if an election office received the ballot.

Texas already provides free voter ID for in-person voting.[105]

Lie: The Texas law punishes election clerks with arrest for any mistakes during the voting process.

Truth: The law would only allow prosecution for someone who intentionally commits or attempts to commit fraud. The law doesn't target honest mistakes for penalties. As with any other prosecution, the burden of proof would have to factor in intent.

Lie: The law will make it more difficult for disabled citizens in Texas to vote.

Truth: The legislation would only require a disabled voter to sign a statement attesting that they are disabled when giving a reason for sending in a mail-in ballot. That's an easy process and does nothing to block access to ballots from disabled people. What Democrats are worried about is more limits on ballot harvesting. One avenue for ballot harvesting schemes was collecting—and potentially intimidating—disabled voters. The same Texas law also protects voters who need assistance from undue influence or intimidation by increasing disclosure requirements for individuals who assist the voter. Also, an election official is the only person other than a relative or caretaker who can assist a voter. The obvious point here is to avoid the paid political operatives from intimidating voters.[106]

Blue State Hypocrisy

Senate Majority Leader Chuck Schumer and Rep. Alexandria Ocasio-Cortez have demanded federal intervention to stop the state election reforms. But if the two are so worried about what they consider restrictions on voting, they should look at their own state. That supposed ban on water is even more restrictive in New York, which prohibits "providing meat, drink, tobacco, refreshment, or other provision with a retail value of more than [$1]" within 100 feet of the entrance to polling places, according to the National Conference of State Legislatures. So, Georgia caught up with both New York and Montana as part of its new election law prohibiting campaign workers from handing out food or drinks to voters standing in line. Georgia's law allows for seventeen days of early in-person voting. New York, by contrast, allows for just ten days of early in-person voting. New York requires voters casting absentee ballots to provide a reason why they can't come to the polls on Election Day. Georgia has no-excuse absentee voting.

It's not just Schumer and AOC who are hypocrites.

The suppression hysteria industrial complex excoriated Iowa Gov. Kim Reynolds for signing legislation to close polls at 8 p.m. rather than 9 p.m. That only means Iowa polls close at the same time as polling places in Vice President Harris's California, President Biden's Delaware, as well as Maryland, Massachusetts, Michigan, Minnesota, Pennsylvania, Rhode Island, and Washington.[107]

As constitutional legal scholar Ilya Shapiro wrote, "But Democratic criticism of Iowa for reducing early voting from 29 to 20 days is disingenuous when the District of Columbia, Delaware, Hawaii, Maryland, New York, and 16 other states all have shorter in-person voting periods."[108]

Biden's home state of Delaware has tougher voting standards than Georgia's new law on many fronts. Delaware passed a law that will allow early in-person voting for the first time in 2022. Moreover, even as Delaware allows it, Georgia will still provide seven more days of early in-person voting than the state the president represented in the Senate from 1973 to 2009.[109]

Meanwhile, the states of California, New Jersey, and Virginia are among the blue states that require an ID number for absentee ballot applications.

Major League Baseball moved its 2021 All-Star Game from Atlanta to Denver to punish Georgia for its new election integrity law. In several respects, however, Colorado's voting laws are stricter. It's not a clear-cut comparison because Colorado mails out ballots to all active voters. But Colorado voter service and polling centers must be open fifteen days before an election, according to the National Conference of State Legislatures, and that's two fewer days than Georgia allows for early in-person voting. Moreover, Colorado's law states, "If you are voting by mail for the first time, you may also need to provide a photocopy of your identification when you return your mail ballot." [110]

In March 2021, chief of the voter suppression hysteria industrial complex Stacey Abrams praised a New Jersey early-voting law despite the fact the New Jersey law provides nine fewer days of early voting than the Georgia law that Abrams has denounced as "Jim Crow 2.0." So, if the Georgia law was Jim Eagle, the New Jersey law is apparently Jim Condor by Biden's reasoning.

While closely contested in a few elections, Minnesota is generally viewed as a blue state, having last gone to a Republican presidential candidate in 1972. It was the lone Democratic holdout when Republican President Ronald Reagan carried forty-nine states in 1984 against Minnesota favorite son Walter Mondale, the state's former US senator and later vice president. Minnesota also already required a driver's license or other ID for absentee ballot verification.

It's clear what red-state efforts to curb the real threat of voting fraud are trying to accomplish: strengthen voter ID, have clean voter lists, and curb vote trafficking. We'll explain all three of those—the problem and solutions—in the following chapters.

Chapter 3

Playing the Race Card on Voter ID

I n 2019, House Majority Whip James Clyburn, a South Carolina Democrat, tweeted, "55 years ago, the 24th Amendment was ratified, eliminating poll taxes. Yet we are still seeing evidence of poll taxes today in the form of voter ID laws. In a democracy such as ours, we must not have any impediments to voting." The point was as obvious as it was absurd: voter ID is racist.

A couple years later, Rep. Burgess Owens, a Utah Republican, who like Clyburn is also an African American, tweeted, "You know what's racist? Assuming because I'm black that 'I just don't have the capability of getting an I-D.'"

Opposing voter ID laws has been core to the Democratic Party's opposition to virtually any secure election laws. While such laws are broadly popular among voters regardless of racial or party affiliation, Democrat politicians engage in racial demagoguery since there are hardly any other grounds to oppose laws that prevent ineligible people from casting votes. For understandable reasons, such arguments have resonance concerning elections, since voter suppression in America has primarily been tied to race. So it's no surprise that voter ID laws are one of the main targets among the Left's claims of voter suppression.

If—as the Left has claimed for decades—voter ID is about voter suppression, then it has been a miserable failure at suppressing the vote. Voter ID laws have made it easier to vote, harder to cheat, and have increased confidence in elections as demonstrated by higher voter participation. Removing voter ID requirements would harm our election system and benefit Democrat machines.

The Left's weeping, wailing, and gnashing of teeth over showing an ID before voting is all for show.

Hillary Clinton spent four years complaining that the 2016 election was stolen from her. She came up with many reasons for her failure over the years, blaming everyone from Russia's dictator Vladimir Putin to former FBI Director James Comey. She also blamed Republicans for voter suppression, specifically in Wisconsin, whose voter ID law, she whined, depressed turnout by two hundred thousand votes. Her evidence for this claim was a study by the liberal group CIVIS USA, commissioned by the Democratic fundraising organization Priorities USA. Both organizations publicly supported Clinton's campaign in 2016 and oppose voter ID measures, so perhaps they were not the most reliable source.

PolitiFact, which typically bends over backward to give every Democrat the benefit of the doubt, said the study was "Mostly False," and that "experts…question the methodology of the report and say there is no way to put a number on how many people in Wisconsin didn't vote because of the ID requirement."[111]

There was, in fact, a downturn in voter turnout in Wisconsin from 2012 to 2016. And Donald Trump's victory in the Badger State was key to his winning the presidential election. But the state's 2016 turnout was still higher than its 2008 turnout—a bit of an anomaly from the national political scene. The US Elections Project ranked Wisconsin as having the fifth highest turnout in the country—more than many of the states that don't have voter ID laws. For instance, New York, a state that Clinton represented in the Senate and that has no voter ID requirement (even though it is stricter with other voting requirements than many red states), had a 59.3 percent turnout, on par with the national average. Wisconsin, by contrast, had a turnout of 69.4 percent.[112] Wisconsin had a high turnout in 2012 as well, and, personal and political views aside, polling showed that Barack Obama was personally more well-liked than either Donald Trump or Hillary Clinton.

Further, nine of the eleven states that added voter ID laws in 2011 had an increase in turnout from the 2012 election to the 2016 election. Conversely, two of the seventeen states that had no voter ID in 2016, along with Washington, DC, finished in the top five.[113]

Voter ID laws can stop multiple types of fraud, such as impersonating another registered voter, preventing noncitizens from voting, and stopping out-of-state residents or someone registered in multiple jurisdictions. Voter ID not only doesn't suppress turnout, it also, since its beginnings, has been recommended by prominent members of both parties and vindicated in court as a way to make our elections more safe and fair. The main source of these recommendations is the Carter-Baker Commission.

"To ensure that persons presenting themselves at the polling place are the ones on the registration list, the Commission recommends that states require voters to use the REAL ID card, which was mandated in a law signed by the President in May 2005," the final report of the Carter-Baker Commission says. "The card includes a person's full legal name, date of birth, a signature (captured as a digital image), a photograph, and the person's Social Security number. This card should be modestly adapted for voting purposes to indicate on the front or back whether the individual is a U.S. citizen. States should provide an [Election Assistance Commission]-template ID with a photo to non-drivers free of charge."

The report underlined that ID was reasonable and ensured security: "The electoral system cannot inspire public confidence if no safeguards exist to deter or detect fraud or to confirm the identity of voters. Photo IDs currently are needed to board a plane, enter federal buildings, and cash a check. Voting is equally important."[114]

States Act to Identify

Some form of voter ID requirements has been used in some jurisdictions since the 1950s. But Indiana became the first state to have to defend its ID law in the Supreme Court. [115]

The Indiana law was challenged, and the case of *Crawford v. Marion County* worked its way to the Supreme Court, which in 2008 upheld Indiana's ID law as constitutional in a 6–3 opinion. The court ruling prompted more states to adopt the practice.[116] Voter ID requirements soon became quite popular in red and purple states. Today, thirty-five states have voter ID laws on the books, according to the National Conference of State Legislatures.[117]

While voter ID was, in theory, a broadly bipartisan, common-sense measure, in practice, Democrat operatives in the spirit of old school machines feared it put them at a political disadvantage at crunch time. So Democrats made it a partisan issue, using their same old arguments: they simply called voter ID requirements racist without bothering to explain.

During the Obama administration, the Justice Department sued in the Fourth Circuit Court of Appeals and seemed to channel Bull Connor by arguing that Black voters are "less sophisticated" and have difficulty knowing how to register and vote. This came despite a lower court determining that Black voters in North Carolina "fared better in terms of registration and turnout rates in 2014, after the new law was implemented, than in 2010, when the old provisions were in place."[118]

The Left has managed to win some victories against ID laws, as federal courts dealt setbacks to voter ID or proof of citizenship laws in Kansas, North Carolina, North Dakota, Texas, and

Wisconsin claiming the laws disenfranchised voters. [119] But the Supreme Court has overwhelmingly upheld most state ID laws in subsequent cases and dismissed charges that such laws were racially discriminatory.

ID Required to Exercise Constitutional Rights

The bulk of states that adopted voter ID laws did so after Republicans' sweeping victory in the 2010 midterms capturing state legislatures. Democrats objected with their usual accusations of racism and voter suppression. Showing some snark, many Republicans responded by chiding the 2012 Democratic National Convention for requiring photo ID to enter the building.

Other proponents of voter ID noted that, without ID, you can't drive a car, fly on a plane, open a bank account, buy alcohol or tobacco products, get an M-rated video game, purchase some prescriptions, or rent a car. But these arguments aren't the strongest defense for voter ID, because there is no constitutional right to attend the Democratic National Convention, fly commercial, get a driver's license, play video games, or even engage in various other financial transactions. Voting, by contrast, is a constitutional right. But federal, state, and local governments have required ID to access other constitutional rights for generations. [120]

Here are seven areas of life that either court decisions or the public have accepted as constitutional rights that carry some ID requirements—including the first two rights in our Bill of Rights.

Right to Travel: While there is no constitutional right to board an airplane per se, the right to travel might fall under public accommodations—a matter settled in the Civil Rights Movement. The Transportation Security Administration requires photo ID for everyone boarding a plane. Freedom of movement has been recognized under the privileges and immunities clause of the Constitution. [121] The Supreme Court determined this as far back as 1869 in *Paul v. Virginia*, a precedent that still holds the "right of free ingress into other states, and egress from them." [122]

Welfare: As for welfare, it might be debatable—particularly for those on the Right—whether anyone has a right to those government benefits. That debate aside, the Supreme Court held in the case of *Goldberg v. Kelly* that welfare recipients are entitled to due process with a hearing before benefits can be terminated.[123] Despite that, several states require some type of proof of identity to collect welfare.[124], [125] Specifically, the states of Massachusetts and Missouri require a photo ID on the electronic benefit cards used for purchases under food stamps or Temporary Assistance for Needy Families expenditures.[126] New York City has a municipal ID program. The city's website says residents will need an ID to "get a job," "cash a check," "open a bank account," and "enter a government building." Further, it says, "To be eligible for some public benefits you need to prove your identity, age and residence."[127]

When Democrats aren't just accusing voter ID supporters of being racist, they generally say that the poor and disabled are the least able of all citizens to access a form of government ID. Yet the poor and disabled are also the most likely to rely on social welfare programs—many of which require some form of ID to access.

Right to Bear Arms: ID is required to exercise the constitutional right to own a gun. Many on the Left would prefer that the Second Amendment not exist, but the Supreme Court clearly affirmed in the 2008 *Heller* decision that the right to bear arms belongs to individuals.[128] Still, the District of Columbia requires gun owners to show ID when buying a gun. They also register those guns and obtain a license for any shotgun, rifle, or handgun.[129], [130] New York City allows the selling of handguns but with stricter rules than New York state. To buy a gun in the city, an individual must appear in person to fill out a seventeen-page handgun purchase authorization form to qualify for a purchase license. The form costs $340 and $89.75 for fingerprinting. The *New York Times* wrote that applicants "must provide an original Social Security card, birth certificate, two recent color photographs and other documents."[131] The application also requires individuals to explain employment dismissal and health history in addition to the background check that all gun buyers go through. Yet New York considers it burdensome to ask someone to take a few moments to show an ID before voting.

Free Speech: It's not just the politically loaded Second Amendment. First Amendment freedoms sometimes require identification—for example, the right to petition your government. Someone who meets with a government official must show a government-issued photo ID. The right to peacefully petition as a professional matter—beyond writing or calling a congressional office—generally requires becoming a registered lobbyist.[132] States have various requirements for registered lobbyists as well.[133] Moreover, the right to peaceably assemble—in a protest march or even a celebratory parade—usually requires a municipal or local government permit.[134]

Marriage: The 1967 *Loving v. Virginia* ruling by the Supreme Court not only struck down bans on interracial marriage but established that under the law marriage is a fundamental right.[135] Every state and most jurisdictions require some official ID to obtain a marriage license. New York City, for example, states, "You and your prospective spouse must have one form of proper identification in order to apply for a Marriage License." This "proper identification" includes a driver's license, active military ID card, passport, or permanent resident card.[136]

So why exactly should the right to vote have a special carveout from this eminently reasonable safeguard?

Well, a Brennan Center for Justice survey—all the way back in 2006 (a year after Carter-Baker but two years before the Supreme Court's decision popularized voter ID)—determined that up to 11 percent of Americans do not have IDs and contended that fees, logistics, and travel impose a deterrence from voting.[137] But we all know where the Brennan Center stands ahead of time. States that adopted voter ID provide it for free, so that argument seems like a tough sell—or a blatant lie to smear election integrity advocates.

Proof That Voter ID Doesn't Suppress the Vote

Since the Supreme Court's 6–3 ruling upholding Indiana's voter ID law in 2008 (at a time when the high court had five conservative and four liberal justices), Democrats have irresponsibly made the comparison of voting laws that they don't like to "Jim Crow."

But few seem to buy the lie. Polls consistently show that about 60 percent of Democrats and about 70 percent of non-white voters support voter ID, and about 80 percent overall back voter ID. Polls also found that big majorities of whites, blacks, and other minorities think it's more important to prevent fraud than to make it easier to vote.[138], [139], [140]

Democrats want the unenlightened masses to repent of those supposedly incorrect, racist opinions—but they shouldn't, because the majority view is the correct one. To look at the factual case in favor of voter ID, let's turn to academia, including Ivy League professors, along with federal government data, neither known for espousing right-wing talking points. The facts show that voter ID not only doesn't suppress votes but that voter turnout is on the rise across all demographics.

A National Bureau of Economic Research study from 2019 examined ten years' worth of turnout data from across the country and concluded that voter ID laws have "no negative effect on registration or turnout overall or for any specific group defined by race, gender, age, or party affiliation."[141] The NBER study, conducted by Enrico Cantoni at the University of Bologna and Vincent Pons at Harvard Business School, found that voter ID laws don't decrease voter turnout, including that of minority voters.[142]

The study also determined ID laws have "no significant effect" on preventing fraud, but prevention-based laws could be based on proving a negative. The bottom line is that, according to the study, voter registration and turnout rates didn't change after voter ID laws were implemented, and there was no statistically observable change in voting behavior before or after. Moreover, it didn't find any impact on states that the Left claims are "purging" voters from the voter lists (a topic that will be addressed in the next chapter). The study noted that Hispanic voter turnout increased in states with voter ID requirements.[143]

Looking back at previous elections, Census Bureau data shows that Black, Hispanic, and Asian voter turnout all increased by double digits from the 2014 midterm to the 2018 midterm election. In Georgia, Black voter turnout was 68.4 percent in 2018—when Stacey Abrams was supposedly robbed—compared to 67 percent among white voters, and overall Black voter registration increased by 6 percent that year.[144]

The Pew Research Center found "historic jumps" in turnout for every racial group in 2018. Black voter turnout rose by 27 percent nationally. Meanwhile, Asian and Hispanic turnout soared by 50 percent.[145]

There was a notable exception to this evidence in favor of voter ID laws: a January 2017 study from professors at the University of California San Diego and Bucknell University purported that ID laws disproportionately affect minorities and "diminish the participation of Democrats and those on the left, while doing little to deter the vote of Republicans and those on the right."[146]

But that one didn't last long. Professors from Yale, Stanford, and the University of Pennsylvania examined the same data and determined the original study had measurement errors and misinterpreted data. The Yale-Stanford-Pennsylvania study found there is "no definitive relationship between strict voter ID laws and turnout."[147]

ID to Absentee Ballots vs. Signature Verification

Most states do not have ID requirements for absentee voting and instead use signature verification. Signature verification is significantly less precise and very subjective compared to ID, which is finite.

Signature verification for absentee ballots can be incredibly difficult. Election workers in some cases might reject a signature unjustifiably. In other cases, election workers moving rapidly through thousands of absentee ballots won't likely spend time on verification. Either way, it can be an arbitrary process. That's why expanding voter ID—meaning adding a driver's license number or the last four digits of a Social Security number to an absentee ballot application—should be adopted in every state. There is nothing arbitrary about ID.

Although ID is more secure, it likely makes disenfranchisement less likely than election workers deciding whether a signature looks correct.

For example, Colorado rejected twenty-nine thousand ballots over signatures that didn't match in 2020.[148] That's not to say the ballots were fraudulent. Signatures can change over time. Just ask Florida Gov. Ron DeSantis. The *Tampa Bay Times* even found that DeSantis's absentee ballot in the 2016 state primary was tossed because an election worker thought his signature didn't quite match.[149]

The Left vs. the World on Voter ID Requirements

The American Left often expresses a deep desire to be more like Europe in every other respect. But strangely, voter ID is an exception. Every European country has voter ID—except for Britain. Closer to home, both Canada and Mexico have voter ID laws. And thirty-three of the thirty-seven members of the Organization for Economic Cooperation and Development have voter ID laws. The exceptions are Britain (again), Japan, New Zealand, and Australia. Further, 74 percent of European countries ban absentee voting for residents, according to a database of global voting rules compiled by the Crime Prevention Research Center, which is run by economist John Lott. Japan, by the way, has its own security measure in place, providing each voter with individual tickets that have bar codes. That would probably come across as a little creepy in the more surveillance-skeptical United States.

New Zealand technically requires an ID with a unique code, but it still allows voting without ID. During the pandemic, Poland allowed a one-time universal mail-in voting, while France had limited exemptions allowing the sick or at-risk to vote by mail. Meanwhile, Australia has generally the weakest voter requirements.[150] Interestingly enough, Australia gave the world the concept of the secret ballot.

It's no wonder that months after the release of the Carter-Baker Commission report in 2005, former President Carter stressed the need for photo IDs and said other countries not known for being examples of democracy had fairer elections than the United States.

"It's disgraceful and embarrassing," the former president said in May 2006. On voter ID, Carter said, "Americans have to remember you have to have the equivalent to what we're requiring to cast a ballot to cash a check or board a plane."[151]

In the American Left vs. the world on voter ID, the overwhelming majority of Americans of every ideology and racial background seem to intuitively take the side of the world because voter ID makes sense. The worst that could be said about it is we don't know how many cases of fraud it prevents. Legitimate research shows it doesn't deter voter turnout. When Americans have more confidence in fair elections, voter turnout won't decrease.

It's evident that those who pine for a return to machine politics expected things to turn out differently. For the Left, this wasn't supposed to happen. In 2020, Democrats used COVID-19 to push for election measures such as universal mail-in voting that they have wanted for decades. After the 2020 election, the machine believed it would easily nationalize election law and didn't anticipate pushback from states expanding the ever-popular voter ID requirements.

In the meantime, Democrat politicians and left-wing advocacy groups increasingly seem desperate. No one simply shouts "racist, racist, racist" because they have a better argument. Thus, elections in almost half the states will be more secure in 2022 and 2024 than in 2020.

Chapter 4

The Dead and Out of Towners: Cleaning Voter Rolls

As of November 2021, Theresa Domasiewicz was still a registered voter in Michigan and would have been 108 years old if she were still alive. Ms. Domasiewicz, however, passed away in 2000 but still remained among 25,975 dead people who remained on the Michigan voter rolls, according to a lawsuit filed in US District Court by the Public Interest Legal Foundation, a conservative government watchdog group.

Michigan isn't alone with this type of problem. Some states are very prolific at complying with the law and properly maintaining their voter lists. But, those who want to remain politically active after their heart stops beating might want to consider locating in states that seem to cater to the deceased voting bloc.

Democrat politicians routinely decry the maintenance of voting lists as a "voter purging." It's not much of a purge when the names being removed from voting lists are either dead or people who moved to another state. But never let facts get in the way of hysteria.

Many left-wing advocacy groups have pushed states to stop participating in the Interstate Voter Registration Crosscheck Program or the Electronic Registration Information Center, which are voluntary programs that allow state election officials to cooperate and compare their statewide voter registration information to determine if voters are registered in more than one state.[152]

The last thing most folks think about if they move to a different state is going to the city or county registrar and canceling their local registration. So, these duplicative registrations don't necessarily indicate fraud. Rather, these names are openings for fraudsters, who could use the names of inactive voters to cast votes.

Stacey Abrams, the losing candidate in the 2018 governor's race and chief spokesperson for the Left's suppression myth, has been the most vocal opponent of "purging" the voter list.

"We have to understand that purging does not simply occur because someone has died or has moved out of the state," Abrams said, noting that her opponent in 2018, Secretary of State Brian Kemp, removed hundreds of thousands of names. "The use of this purging led to a disproportionate number of communities of color being disenfranchised. And many didn't know they were purged until they showed up to vote." [153]

The Brennan Center for Justice has conceded the point that some maintenance is necessary but argues it can be done "irresponsibly." Brennan claims, "Many voters discover they're no longer listed only when they arrive at the polling place." That's also unlikely since most states send at least two notices to the listed address before an inactive voter is removed. Brennan added, "between 2014 and 2016, states removed almost 16 million voters from the rolls—a 33 percent increase over the period between 2006 and 2008. The increase was highest in states with a history of voting discrimination."[154]

To anyone who doesn't trust bureaucracy, mistakenly removing the names of eligible voters would seem like a genuine fear. That, however, overlooks the 2002 Help America Vote Act that allows a voter to cast a provisional ballot if there is question about his or her eligibility. So, there is practically zero chance someone would be turned away or their vote would not be counted. Any election official that turns away a voter without even offering the chance to cast a provisional ballot would be violating federal law. What left-wing propaganda refers to as "purging" voter rolls is, in reality, complying with federal law at a time when many states aren't compliant. The 1993 Voter Registration Act is better known as the Motor Voter Law that allows Department of Motor Vehicle offices to register people to vote. The Motor Voter law also requires states to "conduct a general program that makes a reasonable effort to remove" from the official voter rolls "the names of ineligible voters" who have died or changed residence. Among other things, the NVRA requires those registrations to be canceled when voters fail to respond to address confirmation notices and then fail to vote in the next two general federal elections.

The 2002 Help America Vote Act, a bipartisan law created after the 2000 presidential election, calls for states to create a voter registration database to facilitate data sharing and list maintenance across state lines.[155] HAVA further requires states to report data concerning their removal programs to the Election Assistance Commission. Every few years the EAC publishes this data as part of a report it provides to Congress.[156]

In the Grave and Still Eligible to Vote

Nevertheless, the Left has relentlessly resisted maintenance of voter rolls, even though the chances of anyone removed being disenfranchised are incredibly remote.

The state of Pennsylvania reached a settlement agreement in a federal lawsuit with the Public Interest Legal Foundation in 2021 to remove twenty-one thousand dead people's names from the Keystone State's voter registration lists. The legal foundation provided the Pennsylvania Department of State the names of people who had died before the 2020 election but nevertheless remained on the list. The data showed that 9,212 of these registered voters were dead for at least five years, another 1,990 had been dead for at least ten years, and 197 had been dead for at least twenty years.

Pennsylvania agreed to the legal foundation's request to compare its full list with the Cumulative Social Security Death Index to identify dead people who are still listed are registered voters. The state agreed to order county election commissions to remove the dead people's names. [157]

Separate from the aforementioned Michigan case, the city of Detroit also settled with PILF after the watchdog group found thousands of dead people and duplicate names on Motor City's voter registration rolls. PILF found that in 2016, Detroit had a 106 percent registration rate and found 2,503 dead registrants and 4,788 voters registered more than once in the city. Some of these duplication problems came from married-maiden name conflicts, typos, and the wrong gender designations. The largest irregularity was 16,465 voters with no date showing when they registered to vote. The legal foundation sampled registrants ages eighty-five or older and found more than 2,500 in that age range were listed on the Social Security Death Index. One registered voter was born in 1823—that's before Michigan was part of the United States.[158]

Bureaucratic Incompetence and Outright Corruption

So how do so many ineligible names get on voter registration lists?

Most of it just comes from bureaucrats letting the lists linger without bothering to update them. But fraudsters certainly seize their opportunities from bureaucratic carelessness.

The California state government admitted—after litigation—it mistakenly registered about twenty-five thousand ineligible voters. An example of this came after a Canadian, who is a permanent resident, contacted the *Los Angeles Times* to say he was improperly registered under the state's automatic voter registration system. Then-Secretary of State Alex Padilla said, "persistent errors" will "undermine public confidence."[159]

In 2021, police reported catching Zul Mirza Mohamed—a candidate for mayor of Carrollton, Texas—in the act of stuffing envelopes with absentee ballot applications to Dallas County. But his activities allegedly ran deeper. Investigators determined he forged at least eighty-four voter registration forms. The Texas Attorney General's Office charged him with eighty-four counts of mail ballot fraud. Carrollton, Texas, has a population of 127,279 and spans the counties of Denton, Dallas, and Collin.[160]

In 2021, former Republican Congressman Steve Watkins of Kansas cut a deal to avoid going to trial over voter fraud that he would remain law abiding and pay a $250 fine. Watkins was charged in 2020 for listing a UPS Store as his voting address and then voting in the wrong Topeka City Council race. Prosecutors also charged him with interfering with law enforcement and for lying to Shawnee County detectives.[161]

In 2013, the New York City Department of Investigations called for the New York City Board of Elections to clean up its voter rolls after a sting operation of sorts. The investigators went to the polls signing in with the names of dead people, as convicted felons no longer eligible to vote, or people who had moved out of the city. [162]

In Maryland, Wendy Rosen won the Democratic First Congressional District primary defeating John LaFerla by fifty-seven votes to win the right to challenge Republican Congressman Andy Harris in 2012. However, she was forced to drop out two months before the November election when some Democrats pointed out that she had voted in both Florida and Maryland in 2006 and 2010—duplicate registration that led to double voting by a candidate for office. She was fined $5,000 and sentenced to five hundred hours of community service.[163]

In a 2008 case, Seattle workers with the Association of

Community Organizers for Reform Now, or ACORN, submitted 1,762 fraudulent voter registration forms. ACORN leader Clifton Mitchell was convicted of false registration and served about three months in jail. Four other ACORN colleagues got jail time as well. The state also fined ACORN $25,000 to cover the cost of the investigation. Washington Secretary of State Sam Reed said, "This is the worst case of voter registration fraud in the history of the state of Washington."[164]

"Invitation to Fraud"

After the Motor Voter law and then HAVA came the Carter-Baker Commission report that in 2005 called for states to make it easier to track registered voters who moved from one state to another to reduce duplication of registrations. The report states, "Invalid voter files, which contain ineligible, duplicate, fictional, or deceased voters, are an invitation to fraud.

"In order to assure that lists take account of citizens moving from one state to another, voter databases should be made interoperable between states," the Carter-Baker Commission report says. "This would serve to eliminate duplicate registrations, which are a source of potential fraud."

The 2005 report calls for states to check for ineligible and noncitizens who might be on the voter rolls.

"When an eligible voter moves from one state to another, the state to which the voter is moving should be required to notify the state which the voter is leaving to eliminate that voter from its registration list," the Carter-Baker report says, adding, "All states should have procedures for maintaining accurate lists, such as electronic matching of death records, driver's licenses, local tax rolls, and felon records. Federal and state courts should provide state election offices with the lists of individuals who declare they are non-citizens when they are summoned for jury duty."[165]

Many states took action to clean up voter registration lists, including Ohio, where the law was challenged after the Left claimed this "purging" would cause mass voter suppression. Keep in mind that only until recent elections, Ohio was a battleground state—and both parties were certainly battling over voting procedures. In 2018, in the case of *Husted v. A. Philip Randolph Institute*, the Supreme Court upheld Ohio's procedures for removing the names of voters from their registration lists who have died, moved, or became ineligible for any other reasons. The majority opinion referenced a Pew Research Center study that found "24 million voter registrations in the United States—about one in eight—are either invalid or significantly inaccurate."[166]

The 2012 Pew Center on the States study found more than 1.8 million dead people were still registered to vote, and 2.75 million people were registered in more than one state, while more than seventy-thousand were registered to vote in three or more states.[167] Further, the study estimated about 12.7 million voting records nationwide appeared to be out of date and no longer reflected a voter's current information.[168]

More than 144,000 instances of potential fraud occurred in the 2016 and 2018 elections, according to "Critical Condition," a 2020 report by the Public Interest Legal Foundation. The report says people who voted more than once did so in part because they were registered more than once in the same state or registered in more than one state. Others were recorded as having voted after death[169]

More Voters Than People

A September 2020 study by Judicial Watch, a conservative government watchdog group, asserts that 353 US counties across eight states had 1.8 million more registered voters than eligible voting-age citizens. The states were Alaska, Colorado, Maine, Maryland, Michigan, New Jersey, Rhode Island, and Vermont. They compared the data to the Census Bureau's most recent five-year population estimates from 2014 through 2018. [170]

The state of Pennsylvania and three Pennsylvania counties confessed to having provided inaccurate information to the EAC because of a Judicial Watch lawsuit. Bucks County—with 96 percent voter registration out of all voting-age residents—removed just eight names out of 457,000 registered voters. Chester County—with 97 percent voter registration—removed five from 357,000 registrants, and Delaware County—with 97 percent registration—removed four names out of 403,000 registrations.

These numbers differed from what the state reported. Pennsylvania, in a revised filing, said eighteen other Pennsylvania counties—about one quarter of all the counties—removed fifteen names under the Motor Voter law. In a lawsuit, Judicial Watch found eight hundred thousand inactive voters.[171] Allegheny County removed sixty-nine thousand inactive voters from their lists. The county's election manager, David Voye, said, "I would concede that we are behind on culling our rolls," and that this had "been put on the backburner."[172]

Forty-two Colorado counties—about two-thirds of the state—have voter registration rates that exceed 100 percent of the voting-age population and lead the nation with this problem, according to Judicial Watch.[173] To be clear, exceeding 100 percent means the number of registered voters exceeds the entire county's voting-age population.

In separate research, the Public Interest Legal Foundation found that at least 244 counties across twenty-eight states had bloated voter registration rolls.[174] Moreover, the group determined that 279 counties in thirty-one states had an "implausibly high" 95 percent to 99 percent voter registration rate.[175]

Similarly, in a 2019 assessment, the Public Interest Legal Foundation identified the states with the most problematic counties included red, blue, and battleground states. And it didn't break down neatly along red and blue lines. Kentucky had the most problematic counties with fifty-eight counties. Michigan was a distant second with twenty-nine bloated county voting lists. After that it's South Carolina at twenty-five, Mississippi with twenty-two, Colorado with nineteen, Alabama with fourteen, Illinois with thirteen, South Dakota with eleven, Kansas and Texas with eight each, Nebraska with six, Georgia with five, West Virginia with four, Iowa and Montana with three each, and Missouri, Washington state, and Louisiana each with two counties. Somewhat surprising is that the largest states in the country—California, Texas, Florida, and New York—all of which have had major well-documented voter fraud scandals—have only one county each with bloated voter registration rolls, according to the PILF findings.[176]

On another front, in North Carolina, twenty counties have registration rates that exceed 90 percent of the population, of that, ten counties exceeded 100 percent in 2018. That's compared to the national average of 66.9 percent, according to data from the nonprofit Honest Elections Project.[177] Using EAC data, Judicial Watch also asserts that in nineteen counties in North Carolina, about 20 percent of the registrations were inactive, and 25 percent were inactive in three other counties.[178]

In 2019, Kentucky began cleaning up hundreds of thousands of outdated voter registrations when it entered a consent decree with Judicial Watch over a federal lawsuit.[179] Even California began to remove five million inactive names from its voter lists, the most—1.5 million—from Los Angeles County voter registration rolls after a settlement with Judicial Watch.[180]

Zero Removals Out of Millions of Ineligible Voters

On a similar note, Judicial Watch notified fourteen counties in five states—Arkansas, California, Illinois, New York, and Oregon—there were in evident violation of the Motor Voter law. The review covered November 2016 through November 2020. In this case, the counties appeared not to have removed registrants who failed to respond to address confirmation after failing to vote in multiple elections.

The fourteen counties covering 11.8 million voters had a total of thirty-three voters removed, and of those, five counties removed zero voters. San Bernardino County, California, has 1.3 million registered voters and removed fourteen over the four years. In the same state, Sacramento County has more than one million registered voters but removed zero. In New York, Kings County—the Brooklyn area with 1.7 million registered voters, Queens County with 1.3 million voters, and Nassau County with one million registered voters—removed zero over four years. Only New York County—the Manhattan area—has 1.2 million registered voters and removed two over the four years.[181]

Judicial Watch got the numbers from state reports to the Election Assistance Commission. About 10 percent of Americans move every year in America, but these and other counties don't reflect that, otherwise, they would generate hundreds of thousands of registration cancellations each year, noted Robert Popper, a senior attorney for Judicial Watch.[182]

Interstate Cross Check

This suggests that more states should join interstate cross-check programs to compare state voter rolls and identify duplicate voter registration forms.

"Maintaining an accurate voting roll enfranchises voters because it lowers the likelihood of lines at the polls, reduces voter confusion and decreases the number of provisional ballots," Matthew Masterson, then-chairman of the Election Assistance Commission, wrote in a March 2017 op-ed. "Accurate voting lists means more voters are able to vote and have their votes counted. Updated records allow election administrators to plan, to better manage their budget and poll workers, and to improve voter experience."[183]

The Election Assistance Commission, an agency created by the Help America Vote Act, has endorsed state data sharing with tools such as the Electronic Registration Information Center and the Interstate Crosscheck Program that are used by dozens of states.[184]

In the 1990s and early 2000s, there was a broad consensus that clean voting rolls just made sense. Yet, two decades later, cleaning voter rolls is a drastically partisan issue. Today, following the letter of the law for the National Voter Registration Act of 1993, the Help America Vote Act of 2002, and following the recommendations of the Carter-Baker Commission—and the Supreme Court's ruling in the Ohio case—could get you accused of enforcing Jim Crow 2.0.

Not only is voter fraud more difficult if the voter registration rolls are clean, but clean voter lists would make it easier to determine if vote denial is actually happening.

Chapter 5

The Big Business of Vote Trafficking

Leslie McCrae Dowless Jr. was a convicted felon for committing insurance fraud. Nevertheless, for years numerous political candidates from both parties in North Carolina had turned to him—and his consulting firm Red Dome Group—to try to win elections.

Dowless's past wasn't just consumed with insurance fraud. He had been involved with shady conduct in politics as well—enough so that North Carolina election officials tried to get him prosecuted prior to the 2018 election. Prosecutors didn't indict him though, and this ultimately left him free to corrupt another election—which he obligingly did.[185]

In 2018, Mark Harris, a Republican candidate for North Carolina's Ninth Congressional District seat, hired Dowless's firm to work for his campaign.[186] Early on Mark Harris's son—John Harris—warned his father against bringing Dowless into the campaign because of the previous election shenanigans.[187] Harris clearly should have listened.

Harris beat incumbent Congressman Robert Pittenger in a Republican primary. In a gloomy year for Republicans, Harris went on to defeat his Democrat opponent Dan McCready by 905 votes, about 0.3 percent of the ballots cast that November.[188, 189]

However, the victory would unravel. Although Democrats typically laugh at even the suggestion that mass mail-in voting might be prone to fraud, in this case, North Carolinians and the nation would see Democrats getting a nasty taste of what it's like being on the losing end of fraud. But this didn't rattle the party into any reflection on the issue. Playing the long game, it has doubled down on promoting the fraud-prone practice of ballot harvesting.

The North Carolina State Board of Elections refused to certify the results after evidence of what it called "concerted fraudulent activities related to absentee by-mail ballots." The fraud was heavily about vote trafficking, also known as ballot harvesting, in which third parties, including candidates and political operatives, collect and deliver ballots. The political operatives can go directly to the homes of voters, collect their ballots, and then drop large portions off at the election office.[190] As a rule, the old school machine politics states embrace this practice, and clean election states either ban it or curb it.

Twenty-seven states and the District of Columbia allow third parties to distribute and return ballots, according to CBS News. A dozen—or almost half—of those states put limits on the number of ballots that someone can collect and return for voters. Another ten states allow ballots to be returned only by a voter's family member.[191] The paid operatives are sometimes called "ballot brokers." In Florida, they're known as "boleteros," and in Texas they're called "politiqueras." Both of these states passed laws to ban ballot harvesting after significant scandals.[192, 193]

As it happens, lax laws were not the problem in North Carolina, where the statute says only the voter and "a voter's near relative or the voter's verifiable legal guardian" is allowed to return a completed absentee ballot to election officials. That's why the shady election fraud was caught.[194, 195] One can only imagine how many elections are stolen in states that promote ballot harvesting, with little means of tracking what goes wrong.

The North Carolina election board's investigation determined that absentee ballot "requests were fraudulently submitted under forged signatures, including a deceased voter." The final report says that Dowless paid people to "collect absentee request forms, to collect absentee ballots, and to falsify absentee ballot witness certifications." His employees were compensated based on how many absentee ballots they collected. So, corrupt incentives were built in.[196]

Operating like the golden era of Tammany Hall that knew how to find voters, the ballot request forms were usually photocopied so Dowless could find the voters for the next election. The elections board report says that since Dowless "maintained photocopies of completed absentee by mail request forms from prior elections—including voters' signatures and other information used to verify the authenticity of a request—Dowless possessed the capability to submit forged absentee ballots by mail request forms without voters' knowledge and without detection by elections officials."[197]

Dowless and his employees went to voters' homes after absentee ballots had been delivered to collect the ballots. They would often sign as witnesses regardless of whether they saw the voter sign the ballots, and they pressured voters to vote for Harris. The Dowless employees collected other ballots that were not completed, and Dowless and his staff would fill out the blank ballots from his home or office, according to the findings of the election board. One of Dowless's staffers forged her mother's name as a witness on absentee-ballot envelopes.[198]

Dowless was clearly no rookie and took some painstaking precautions such as delivering a few absentee ballots to the post office at a time and making sure the ballots were mailed from post offices geographically close to where the voter lived—or in some cases where the ballot had been stolen. The false witnesses would also ensure they signed the same dates as the voters' signature and signed with the same color ink.

Despite being so precise in these areas, and as well financed as the operation was, the Dowless team was still sloppy enough to get caught by laymen rather than election officials or law enforcement. Several voters discovered that absentee ballot request forms "were submitted on their behalf, but without their knowledge, consent, or signature," according to the board's report.[199]

Dowless didn't agree to testify to the board of elections unless they granted him immunity. The board declined and further accused him of "witness tampering and intimidation" to obstruct the investigation.[200] Dowless's stepdaughter—Lisa Britt—testified to the board that she helped to fill out blank and incomplete ballots for Republican candidates.[201]

For his part, Mark Harris, who denied knowing what Dowless was doing, admitted a new election should be held—and declined to run in it. Harris never faced charges, and we can only go by the evidence that came forward. But hiring Dowless clearly showed bad judgment.[202]

After an investigation that included 142 voter interviews, the board ended up voiding the Harris victory as well as voiding two other local elections. It ordered a new special election. The board determined Dowless ran the fraud scheme that was "enabled by a well-funded and highly organized criminal operation."

Reminder, most Democrats say large-scale organized fraud operations are imaginary. The board further determined the election "was corrupted by fraud, improprieties, and irregularities so pervasive that its results are tainted as the fruit of an operation manifestly unfair to the voters and corrosive to our system of representative government." Because of the "coordinated, unlawful, and well-funded absentee ballot scheme" that "perpetrated fraud and corruption upon the election," the state Board of Elections ordered a new election. The members determined it wasn't possible to "determine the precise number of ballots" affected by the fraud and whether it determined the outcome.[203, 204]

Democratic Gov. Roy Cooper praised the board and asserted, "This action sends a strong message that election fraud must not be tolerated."[205] After the scandal, the Republican-controlled North Carolina state legislature passed a law to make names of individuals who requested absentee ballots confidential and passed harsher penalties for violating the existing anti-vote trafficking law.[206]

A Wake County grand jury indicted Dowless in February 2019 for obstruction of justice, conspiracy to obstruct justice, possession of absentee ballots, and perjury in connection to both the 2016 general election and 2018 primary election. Another superseding indictment in July 2019 added perjury and solicitation of perjury. Six of Dowless's employees were also charged with crimes.[207] It got worse in April 2020 when federal prosecutors charged Dowless with Social Security fraud because he allegedly received disability benefits at the same time he was getting $130,000 in political consulting fees.[208] However, in April 2022, Dowless died of lung cancer before going to trial. [209]

Republican Dan Bishop won the September 2019 special election over McCready. That McCready would lose the special election after being so obviously wronged in such a clear and convincing way in the regular election suggests that maybe Harris could have won without cheating had he and his surrogates not allowed themselves to be blinded by ambition. If he had still lost, well, life would have gone on, but Harris would have at least been an also-ran without the taint of corruption over his campaign.

This case and others prove that a well-funded, well-organized plot to steal an election can occur. It was stopped in this case—but the fact is that what went on in North Carolina isn't entirely illegal in other states. Yes, outright forgery and voter intimidation are outlawed virtually everywhere. But laws that specifically allow ballot harvesting invite such practices. It's quite clear that Harris wasn't that far from pulling this fraudulent victory off.

Promoting Trafficking

Here again, it's worth returning to the 2005 Carter-Baker Commission recommendations.

"Absentee ballots remain the largest source of potential voter fraud," the Carter-Baker Commission report says. "State and local jurisdictions should prohibit a person from handling absentee ballots other than the voter, an acknowledged family member, the U.S. Postal Service, or other legitimate shipper, or election officials. The practice in some states of allowing candidates or party workers to pick up and deliver absentee ballots should be eliminated."

Another nonpartisan source, the Election Assistance Commission, warned in 2006: "One point of agreement is that absentee voting and voter registration by nongovernmental groups create opportunities for fraud. For example, a number of studies cited circumstances in which voter registration drives have falsified voter registration applications or have destroyed voter registration applications of persons affiliated with a certain political party. Others conclude that paying persons per voter registration application creates the opportunity and perhaps the incentive for fraud."[210]

During the COVID-19 pandemic, after some prodding from Democrats in the lead-up to the 2020 election and frequent reference to the 2005 report, former President Jimmy Carter issued a statement saying, "I urge political leaders across the country to take immediate steps to expand vote-by-mail and other measures that can help protect the core of American democracy—the right of our citizens to vote."[211]

Many of the states that passed election reform laws in 2021—such as Georgia and Florida—banned ballot trafficking. Many other states banned the risky and reckless practice in previous years.

Democrats not only are ambivalent about voter fraud, they are apparently also entirely OK with voter intimidation.

HR 1, the wish list bill of election proposals that Democrats call the "For the People Act," mandates no-fault absentee ballots, bans witness signatures or notarization requirements for absentee ballots, and forces states to accept absentee ballots up to ten days after Election Day if those ballots are postmarked by Election Day, which the legislation casts as "prohibiting states from imposing restrictions on an individual's ability to vote by mail."[212]

Worst of all, the HR 1 language benignly states, "The State... shall permit a voter to designate any person to return a voted and sealed absentee ballot to the post office, a ballot drop-off location, tribally designated building, or election office so long as the person designated to return the ballot does not receive any form of compensation based on the number of ballots that the person has returned and no individual, group, or organization provides compensation on this basis; *and may not put any limit on how many voted and sealed absentee ballots* [emphasis added] any designated person can return to the post office, a ballot drop off location, tribally designated building, or election office."

At least prohibiting paying per ballot will not legally endorse the perverse incentives for cheating. But "designated" is such a whitewashed term when political operatives show up at someone's door. And zero limits on the number of ballots that can be collected by a single trafficker is clearly asking for trouble. The preying and intimidation from this practice are obvious. To nationalize a practice that led to overturning a recent congressional race—one that harmed the Democratic candidate at that—is outrageous. But much like Tammany Hall, the Daley machine, and the Pendergasts, Democrats are thinking about the long war.

There was plenty of warning before November 2020—when 64 percent of ballots came in after Election Day—that mail-in voting would be problematic.

In May 2020, allegations of absentee ballot fraud flew out of Paterson, New Jersey, where the state attorney general charged four people—including a city councilman—with crimes.[213] Nevertheless, that same year, New Jersey Governor Phil Murphy ordered that 6.3 million 2020 ballots will be mailed in.[214] Also during the 2020 primary season, five hundred thousand ballots were rejected across twenty-three states—one in four of those were from battleground states.[215]

Of the twenty-seven states that expressly allow a third party to deliver ballots, thirteen states don't specify who can deliver another voter's ballot—leaving it accessible for political operatives.

It's not difficult to find other examples of elections overturned because of vote trafficking scandals.

The East Chicago Way

In the 2003 mayor's race in East Chicago, Indiana, challenger George Pabey had a 199-vote election night lead over eight-term incumbent Mayor Robert Patrick. But after 278 absentee votes came in, it appeared the incumbent was the winner.[216]

Local political operative Allan "Twig" Simmons, working for the mayor, convinced voters in the city to allow him to fill out their absentee ballots in exchange for jobs. Simmons ended up pleading guilty and was sentenced to three years of probation and one hundred hours of community service.

The trial lasted a week and a half and included 165 witnesses. The judge determined the mayor's allies "perverted the absentee voting process and compromised the integrity and results of that election." The judge found "direct, competent, and convincing evidence that established the pervasive fraud, illegal conduct, and violations of elections law" that proved the "voluminous, widespread and insidious nature of the misconduct."[217]

In a scam that involved vote buying, voter intimidation, and phony absentee voter application forms, the fraud led to at least seven convictions or guilty pleas by 2008. When the case made its way to the Indiana Supreme Court, the state's high court said a new election was "compelled" because "a deliberate series of actions occurred making it impossible to determine the candidate who received the highest number of legal votes cast in the election."[218]

Voting Vice in Miami

In 2012, a Miami-Dade County Grand Jury issued a special report that called for the Florida legislature to ban anyone from being "in possession of more than two absentee ballots at one time" unless the ballots are "those of the voter and members of the voter's immediate family." The report continues, "once that ballot is out of the hands of the elector, we have no idea what happens to it. The possibilities are numerous and scary."

The report came after several arrests over absentee ballot fraud in the 2012 primary in Miami. A computer program automatically sent in bogus absentee ballot applications to the Miami-Dade County Department of Elections. Also, "boleteros" dropped off absentee ballots at the district office of a sitting member of the Miami-Dade Board of County Commissioners.

It turned out 150 absentee ballots were initially dropped off at a county commissioner's office, collected by the commissioner's aide, then dropped off in a single mailbox. A postal carrier discovered these ballots and reported them, which led to multiple arrests. There wasn't clear evidence this scam changed election outcomes, but it harkened back to the corrupt 1997 mayor's race where absentee fraud did. The grand jury in 2012 noted the fact this was still happening required new laws. The grand jury report states: "In 1997, the City of Miami had one of its most memorable elections. The mayoral election for that year was plagued with widespread absentee ballot fraud. Many absentee ballots were filled out by boleteros.... Fast forward to the 2012 primary election and we are faced...with numerous allegations of absentee ballot fraud and several arrests."[219]

In 1997, Miami Mayor Joe Carollo won overwhelmingly in a five-way race with in-person voting, but it was not quite a majority.[220] So, the November 4 contest went into a runoff on November 13, in which his opponent, Xavier Suarez, got two-thirds of the absentee votes and won the election—or so it seemed. Law enforcement found evidence of at least five thousand fraudulent absentee ballots.[221]

Fifty-four people were convicted in the voting fraud case, including a Miami City commissioner charged with being accessory after the fact to voter fraud, the commissioner's chief of staff, and the chief of staff's father, according to the Miami-Dade County grand jury report.[222]

Investigators found the overall 1997 scam involved stolen ballots, false registration addresses, false witnessed ballots, and hundreds of ballots illegally cast obtained by twenty-nine "ballot brokers" who invoked their right not to testify to avoid self-incrimination.[223] During the scheme, volunteers pressured elderly food stamp recipients into voting.

The *Miami Herald* won a Pulitzer Prize in 1999 for uncovering the election wrongdoing.[224] The newspaper told the story of a seventy-year-old woman recovering from a stroke at a hospital who said she was reportedly badgered by the harvesters to vote for Suarez. There were other stories of seniors in hospitals and nursing homes being taken advantage of.[225]

The trial court ordered a new election, but the appeals court ruled the city shouldn't bother and overturned the election, reinstating Carollo as mayor. The appeals court ruled that given such "massive absentee voter fraud" the bests solution was "to not encourage such fraud" by holding a new election.

"[W]ere we to approve a new election as the proper remedy following extensive absentee voting fraud, we would be sending out the message that the worst that would happen in the face of voter fraud would be another election," the appeals court said.[226]

Absentee ballots have always been the most vulnerable for tampering or just getting lost. Going back to 1998 after the scandalous Miami election, a report from the Florida Department of

Law Enforcement determined the "lack of 'in-person, at-the-polls' accountability makes absentee ballots the 'tool of choice' for those inclined to commit voter fraud."[227]

Fresno Fraud

Even California lawmakers—at one point—thought it sensible that only relatives or someone living in the household should be allowed to return ballots. But the state with one-party Democrat rule made room for political operatives to ensure it remains a one-party state. The California law is framed as allowing the voter to "designate any person to return the ballot." As if the voter always has that unilateral choice free of coercion or intimidation to "designate" someone.[228]

California Gov. Jerry Brown signed Assembly Bill 1921 to legalize ballot harvesting in 2016 to take effect in the 2018 election.[229] The new law said political operatives could be paid for collecting ballots, but the pay thankfully couldn't be based on the number of ballots they collect. Still, one must wonder how well that is policed.[230]

In a sneak preview of the 2020 election, several House Republican candidates out of California led on election night, but their lead evaporated as the mail-in ballots came in the following weeks. Even Democrat supporters called this a slow-rolling blue wave, as Democrats racked up more victories as times passed. The most glaring example was the one-time GOP stronghold of Orange County, where every seat went Democrat after 250,000 absentee ballots were dropped off, according to the *San Francisco Chronicle*.[231]

In passing this trafficking law, California lawmakers apparently forgot about the Fresno County, California, school board election of 1991. The state Supreme Court eventually overturned the outcome in the 1993 case of *Gooch v. Hendrix*. This case and others indeed show minority communities or marginalized groups are potentially the most likely victims of ballot trafficking schemes.[232]

The Voter Education Project for the Fresno Chapter of the Black American Political Association of California, also known as BAPAC, delivered absentee ballots for thirteen targeted seats on the county's school board.

Before the case reached the state Supreme Court, the trial court heard testimony that BAPAC's operatives visited people's homes to get them to either register to vote or to fill out an absentee ballot application form. The catch was the absentee ballots would be sent to the BAPAC office instead of directly to the voters' addresses.

BAPAC staff delivered ballots to the voters' homes, where voters were "encouraged to vote in the presence" of BAPAC ballot harvesters. A jury heard one witness say three BAPAC personnel came to his home late at night and "told him for whom to vote" and were "emphatic that he not seal his ballot." Another witness said a BAPAC staffer visited his home and filled out an absentee ballot in his name without his permission.

Fresno County election officials sent 1,300 supposedly requested ballots to BAPAC's address. Of those, 269 were not returned. Out of the 1,023 sent in, sixty-three were disqualified for invalid signatures that didn't match the signature on file. The county disqualified another ninety-three absentee ballots because of fraud and tampering. The rest of the ballots were tossed because of other assorted illegal conduct, largely on BAPAC using its address for delivery of the absentee votes.

The California Supreme Court determined the election had "widespread illegal voting practices that permeated this election—including fraud and tampering" with absentee ballots and other "illegal votes affected the outcomes of the consolidated elections."[233]

Texas-Sized Problems

It wasn't just the biggest blue state that showed the potential for problems. The largest red state in the nation certainly had problems before banning ballot harvesting. Texas is a state that has had a shabby record of corruption before reforms in recent years. Texas passed a law signed by Gov. Greg Abbott in September 2017 to make it a first-degree felony to engage in organized election fraud that would include the "intent to establish, maintain or participate in a vote harvesting organization."

In early 2019, the first case was prosecuted when Edinburg Mayor Richard Molina and eighteen others were charged in a voter fraud ring. Molina was acquitted in August 2022. At least Texas has a decent record of prosecuting these cases.

In 2016, former Weslaco city commissioner Guadalupe Rivera pleaded guilty to one count of providing illegal "assistance" to a voter in a 2013 race he won by sixteen votes. Rivera admitted to filling out an absentee ballot "in a way other than the way the voter directed or without direction from the voter." A judge determined that thirty ballots were cast illegally and ordered a new election, which Rivera lost. He initially faced sixteen related charges, but fifteen were dropped as part of a plea deal. He was sentenced to a year of probation and ordered to pay a $500 fine.[234]

In 2014, in what was called an "unlikely alliance" with Tea Party group Direct Action Texas, a former Democrat state representative was defeated in the March 2014 primary by 111 votes and several Democrat consultants teamed to review applications for absentee ballots. They found the applications had each name and address written in identical handwriting.[235]

Overturned for Ballot Harvesting

More recent local elections were upended after shenanigans involving ballot trafficking.

In 2017, in Eatonville, Florida, Mayor Anthony Grant was convicted of a felony charge of voting fraud and misdemeanor absentee voting violations. Prosecutors said that as a candidate in 2015, Grant coerced absentee voters to cast ballots for him.

In at least one case, prosecutors said, Grant personally solicited an absentee vote from a nonresident. Grant, a former mayor, lost the in-person vote but won the election with more than twice the number of absentee ballots that incumbent Bruce Mount got. After Grant's indictment, then-Gov. Rick Scott suspended the mayor. After his conviction, he was sentenced to four hundred hours of community service and four years' probation.[236]

New York State Assembly candidate Hector Ramirez pleaded guilty to one count of criminal possession of a forged instrument during his 2014 campaign. Prosecutors charged Ramirez with deceiving voters into giving their absentee ballots to his campaign on the false premise that it would submit them. Instead, Ramirez's campaign inserted his name on at least thirty-five absentee ballots, prosecutors said. Ramirez initially won, but a recount determined that he lost by two votes. Bronx Supreme Court Justice Steven Barrett ruled that Ramirez could not run for office again for three years.[237]

In clear abuse of local government power in Martin, Kentucky, Mayor Ruth Robinson, her husband, and her sons were all convicted of voter fraud after they intimidated poor and disabled citizens living in public housing and in properties that Robinson owns into voting for her on absentee ballots in the 2014 election—some of which Robinson herself had filled out. At the properties she owns, prosecutors determined Mayor Robinson threatened to evict residents if they didn't vote for her. The family members offered bribes to others for buying votes. She was sentenced to ninety months in prison.[238, 239]

What the Supreme Court Had to Say

Arizona's 2016 law made ballot trafficking a class 6 felony. The state already had an existing law that said if an Arizona voter tried to vote out-of-precinct, he or she is redirected to the proper precinct—or cast a provisional ballot if they prefer. The Democratic National Committee claimed both laws disproportionately harmed minority voters and sued Arizona, claiming the law violated the 1965 Voting Rights Act. Democrats argued unsuccessfully that the state law was preempted by federal laws regulating the US Postal Service, violated the First Amendment rights of the ballot collector to engage in political speech, and was an unconstitutionally vague criminal statute.[240]

In July 2021, the Supreme Court upheld in a 6–3 ruling that the Arizona ballot harvesting and out-of-precinct voting policies don't violate Section 2 of the Voting Rights Act. In the case of *DNC v. Brnovich*, named for Arizona Attorney General Mark Brnovich, the high court's opinion asserted that a disparate impact analysis isn't significant enough to prevent states from running their own elections. Rather, the court held there must be a connection between a state election practice and the actual denial of the right to vote. Section 2 prohibits voting practices or procedures that discriminate based on race, color, or language minority group.[241]

Just as the Supreme Court's 6–3 ruling in 2008 made elections more trustworthy by allowing voter ID laws, the high court 6–3 ruling in 2021 on ballot harvesting also made elections more secure. Both are still state decisions, and the modern-day Tammany heirs are fighting this every step. Ultimately, we are not talking about a zero-sum game. Election integrity measures—if properly executed and understood—should be about ensuring every legally, eligible voter is able to vote, but only legal and eligible voters do vote.

The scary predictions that Democrats made about voter ID laws passed in the early 2000s and in 2011 after Republicans swept state houses never came true. In most cases, voter turnout increased. The state laws enacted in 2021, and some in 2022, ensured a return mostly to pre-COVID-19 era voting. It's clear Democrat politicians didn't want a crisis—that conveniently fell in an election year—to go to waste. Yet, even recognizing the opportunism, we can all recognize that 2020 posed extraordinary circumstances. The country should not be facing a crisis situation in future elections.

What the Left found controversial in the state bills was broadly popular with the American public. The biggest problem is likely that such election security measures weren't adopted in more states.

Democrat propaganda claims the GOP would end elections as we know them through state reforms. In reality, legislation such as HR 1, correctly nicknamed the "Corrupt Politicians Act," would be a far greater abuse, as will be explained. The Democrats have had a long history of corrupt practices, be it Jim Crow or Tammany Hall. The party's current-day legislative agenda builds on that.

PART TWO

Uncomfortable Truths about the 2020 Election

This tumultuous pandemic-riddled year was ending with a close presidential election made even more stressful by the slow-rolling results. After days of counting ballots in an election outcome that was unclear, the candidate the media identifies as the apparent loser of the 2020 election steps to the podium and shocks Americans as he refuses to concede. He says his supporters won't allow him to bow out, alleges a dishonest election, and vows to fight on.

Next, he calls on governors of his own party from states his opponent won to intervene and certify their state's Electoral College votes in his favor.

No, this wasn't Donald Trump. This was Joe Biden's message. Actually, it was Hillary Clinton's 2016 campaign chairman John Podesta role-playing Biden in a war games session from the "Transition Integrity Project" run by several mostly well-known Democrat operatives and a few Never Trump Republicans. Under the scenario, Podesta as Biden convinced three Democrat governors of Trump-won states to send pro-Biden electors to the Electoral College. The *New York Times* reported in August 2020 on the Transition Integrity Project that under this wargame: "The House named Mr. Biden president; the Senate and White House stuck with Mr. Trump. At that point in the scenario, the nation stopped looking to the media for cues, and waited to see what the military would do."[242]

The Transition Integrity Project included three other scenarios. The point here is that while Donald Trump and some on his legal team did some reprehensible and irresponsible things in the post-election, no one should forget that pre-election, Biden supporters were saying insane things as well. Hillary Clinton said Biden should "not concede under any circumstances" if Trump is victorious. Democrats in Congress were claiming the US Postal Service was plotting to steal the election on Trump's behalf.

Under a counterfactual Trump victory in 2020, there's no way to know if Biden would have followed the advice of either Clinton or Podesta had he lost. But it's not unreasonable to anticipate the party would have called an insurance policy to attempt to ensure Trump didn't have another four years.

Interestingly, a Politico Morning Consult poll found that before the 2020 elections, 52 percent of Democrats believed the presidential election would not be free and fair. For Republicans, only 35 percent were skeptical about the election being free and fair. Days after the networks called the election for Biden, 70 percent of Republicans said the election was not free and fair, while 95 percent of Democrats were confident it was a free and fair election.[243]

As one participant in the Transition Integrity Project correctly told the *Boston Globe*, "There is a narrative among activists in both parties that the loss must be illegitimate."[244]

The Transition Integrity Project's counterfactual sort of tells us Democrats are good at planning. The real story of the 2020 election is perhaps an even better indication of how good Democrats are at planning. The wild changes in state election laws, the mass mail-in voting—historically the largest source of fraud—and the spike in ballot harvesting were all longstanding goals of the party that just needed a preface to implement them. On top of that, a tech billionaire privately funded election administration that resulted in a government-sanctioned Democrat get-out-the-vote campaign.

The 2020 election revealed Democrats used a pandemic to put in place election policies they have always wanted. Even worse, this established precedents for future elections. A liberal *Time* magazine writer even openly boasted in glowing terms about how a "shadow campaign" of assorted nonprofits and corporations succeeded in ousting Trump. "That's why the participants want the secret history of the 2020 election told, even though it sounds like a paranoid fever dream—a well-funded cabal of powerful people, ranging across industries and ideologies, working together behind the scenes to influence perceptions, change rules and laws, steer media coverage and control the flow of information," *Time*'s Molly Ball wrote.[245]

There are quite a few uncomfortable truths about the 2020 election that would be cold water in the face of some in both political camps.

Joe Biden defeated Donald Trump in the presidential race with an Electoral College victory of 306 to 232 after winning Arizona, Georgia, and Wisconsin by 0.6 percentage points or less. A *Washington Post* analysis in February 2021 found that flipping fewer than forty-three thousand votes across those three states could have likely changed the election outcome by sending the election to the House of Representatives, where Republicans hold a majority of state delegations.

Nevertheless, there is another uncomfortable truth. While a number of things about 2020 seemed fishy, as of this writing almost two years after the 2020 election, there has been no adjudicated evidence that vote totals were altered or that fraud was determinative in delivering the Electoral College or the seven million popular vote victory to Biden. Perhaps there will be, as Trump supporters have contended the matter hasn't fully been investigated.

However, after the 2016 election, a common trope among Democrats—several I know on a friendly level—insisted that Russia made Trump president. Russians clearly meddled in the campaign that year with Facebook ads and hacking. But when I would ask Democrats if there were any evidence this influenced the outcome of the election—the common response was: Well, I just think it's obvious.

Similarly, ask some Trump supporters for clear-cut evidence that Biden's victory was illegitimate. The answer is too often: Well, I just think it's obvious.

"Well, I just think it's obvious" doesn't cut it from a legal standpoint and shouldn't from a journalistic standpoint (though it clearly did for much of the mainstream media during the Trump presidency).

As noted in earlier chapters, many past elections were legitimately overturned because of fraud. There are almost certainly many other elections where the fraudsters successfully stole it and got away with it. But voter fraud is much like any other crime. In America, we need proof and due process. Short of that, it's unhealthy for half the country to view the elected president as illegitimate, be it Trump or Biden.

The problem is the 2020 election has become a forbidden discussion, largely because of the violent January 6 riot, and partly because Trump and his legal team tossed around outlandish claims and thus made it very easy for the Left to lump every legitimate question and clear irregularity into a giant pot they called the "Big Lie."

Although the full story of the 2020 election hasn't been told, subsequent investigations have provided noteworthy discoveries. Trump has then overplayed the significance of each new discovery as absolute proof that he was the real winner—which the discoveries don't prove. Democrats and the media use Trump's overstatements as an excuse to scoff and ignore credible findings that don't meet their narrative. And political tribalism continues to be cemented while intellectual curiosity is repelled.

The point is not to dwell on the past but to look at a factual review of findings that should cause concern that we don't see this occur in future elections.

The Wolf of Voting Laws

To prevent another debacle that we saw in 2020, state legislatures need to stop future governors or secretaries of state from unilaterally changing or just setting aside election laws. The worst example of this was in Pennsylvania.

In Pennsylvania, 2.5 million people voted by mail in 2020. In January 2022, the Pennsylvania Commonwealth Court determined the state law that allowed no-excuse mail-in voting during that election was unconstitutional. Further, the court's opinion said, "A constitutional amendment must be presented to the people and adopted into our fundamental law before legislation authorizing no-excuse mail-in voting can be placed upon our statute books."[246]

None of that happened for the presidential race.

This was the fourth closest state in the nation (Arizona, Georgia, and Wisconsin being the others). Biden won Pennsylvania by some eighty thousand votes, likely too big of a gap to have been manipulated. Nevertheless, this was the most egregious example of changing the election rules on a whim. The Pennsylvania statute says that absentee ballots must be postmarked and received no later than 8 p.m. on Election Day. Democratic Gov. Tom Wolf wanted to allow ballots to be counted as long as they arrived by November 6—three days after the election. The Republican-controlled legislature passed a bill that requires voters request a ballot fifteen days before Election Day, as opposed to the existing law of seven days before the election to give mail carriers and election workers a means to deal with the influx. Wolfe said he would veto the Republican proposal.

The Republicans wouldn't pass Wolf's proposal. It likely would have been fitting if they could have hatched a deal. Some states have laws that allow a late arriving absentee ballot to be

counted—so long as it's postmarked by Election Day. Pennsylvania didn't. The legislature didn't pass the bill, and the governor
didn't sign such a law. No matter, the state's partisan elected
state Supreme Court decided in a 4–3 decision to allow mail-in
votes to be counted that arrive by November 6. The justices even
one-upped Wolf, declaring that if postmarks or dates are missing
or illegible, the ballots would be "presumed to have been mailed
by Election Day" unless evidence shows otherwise. When the
Supreme Court essentially enacted Wolf's proposal, there was no
point in negotiating a legislative solution. The point here is that
whether it changes the result or not—this is no way to enact election laws.[247]

"Unlawful" Ballot Drop Boxes

In Wisconsin, where the election was decided by about twenty-one
thousand votes, the state Supreme Court determined in July 2022
that the widely used ballot drop boxes—an accompanying ballot
harvesting—from 2020 were "unlawful."

Heavily Democratic Madison and Milwaukee each had more
than a dozen such ballot drop boxes. [248]

Wisconsin law requires absentee ballots be delivered either
by mail or by personally delivering to the municipal clerk.
Specifically, the statute says: "The legislature finds that voting
is a constitutional right, the vigorous exercise of which should
be strongly encouraged. In contrast, voting by absentee ballot is
a privilege exercised wholly outside the traditional safeguards of
the polling place."

Neither the state legislature nor even the Wisconsin Elections
Commission approved ballot drop boxes. Rather, state bureaucrats working for the commission—not members of the bipartisan commission—issued memos to "authorize municipal clerks
and local elections officials to establish ballot drop boxes." These
staffers also endorsed ballot harvesters, or "agents," to collect and
deliver the ballots to the drop boxes.

The state's high court, in a 4-3 majority ruling, says: "If the right to vote is to have any meaning at all, elections must be conducted according to law. The right to vote presupposes the rule of law governs elections. If elections are conducted outside the law, the people have not conferred their consent upon the government. Such elections are unlawful, and their results are illegitimate."

"Unlawful" and "illegitimate."

Even Trump critic Quin Hillyer, a *Washington Examiner* columnist, wrote: "If former President Donald Trump and his minions dangerously transgressed the second part of that equation by trying to run roughshod over dozens of court decisions and determinations by Trump's own attorney general, the political Left all too often ignores the first part of that equation. It repeatedly tries to make up voting rules on the fly and then justifies them not with reference to statutory language, but instead with ever-more-creative appeals to some sense of cosmic fairness divorced from the laws the people's representatives have made." [249]

Unknown Ballots and Comparing Precincts

With all the Democrat rhetoric about suppression and disenfranchisement, they showed little concern that nearly fifteen million mail-in or absentee ballots were unaccounted for in the 2020 election—and more than one million were undeliverable, according to the Public Interest Legal Foundation, which used data from the Election Assistance Commission.[250]

The PILF report found that 1.1 million mail-in ballots were undeliverable for various reasons and that election officials rejected another 560,814 mail-in ballots. Another 14.7 million mailed ballots met an "unknown" fate, the legal foundation report says.[251]

Los Angeles County had the highest number of "unknown" ballots in 2020, according to the PILF study. It was followed by Clark County, Nevada. Of the ten counties with the most "unknown" ballots, seven are in California, a state that Biden won handily.[252]

In 2020, many officials across the nation boosted mail-in ballots, citing the COVID-19 pandemic. Because of this, the number of lost ballots doubled or nearly doubled in most categories from the last presidential election, the legal foundation's report found.[253] The number of "unknown" ballots almost tripled, from 5.9 million in 2016, according to the PILF report.[254]

Economist John R. Lott Jr. took a novel look at the 2020 vote in a peer-reviewed article published in the journal *Public Choice* that compares mail-in voting from precincts in counties with fraud allegations to mail-in voting to adjacent precincts in counties with no fraud allegations. Such precincts can include the same neighborhood and are usually homogeneous areas with similar demographics and fewer than one thousand voters each. Thus, two adjacent precincts would not normally represent any radical change.[255]

However, the adjacent precincts were anything but homogeneous in the mail-in voting, according to the study by Lott, president of the Crime Prevention Research Center, a former senior advisor for research and statistics at the US Department of Justice's Office of Legal Policy, whose academic career includes working at Yale, Stanford, and the University of Chicago.

His report finds evidence of about 255,000 excess votes—and as many as 368,0000—for Biden in the swing states where the Trump campaign alleged fraud—Arizona, Georgia, Michigan, Nevada, Pennsylvania, and Wisconsin—based on the precinct comparisons. Biden won those five states by a total of 312,253 votes.[256]

Campaigns try to win states, larger regions, or at least multiple counties. So, it seems odd that any campaign would simply sway the voters of one precinct in big numbers to vote one way, while neighbors with the same demographic and socioeconomic makeup—often across the street—vote in different patterns. Yet, that's what the precinct comparisons found.

Zuckerbucks and Government-Sanctioned Democrat Get Out the Vote Campaign

The thought of government institutions working hand-in-glove with a private political group bankrolled by an oligarch to ensure a certain maximum turnout to favor one party certainly comes close to the spirit of Tammany Hall tactics.

American elections shouldn't be bankrolled by billionaires of either side. Facebook founder Mark Zuckerberg poured about $400 million of his personal fortune into local election administration. This resulted in helping drive up the Democrat voter participation. Conservatives didn't like this. But it's quite likely Democrats would not be happy if Koch Industries, or any billionaire on the right, used their fortune to push government operations to drive up the vote in Republican areas.[257]

Zuckerberg's $350 million in donations to the Center for Tech and Civic Life went to local election offices to be used as COVID-19 relief funds, supposedly to make voting safer. But the grants went disproportionately to Democrat-leaning jurisdictions. With regards to safety, almost none of the money was used for personal protective equipment.[258]

A breakdown of the money indicates these "Zuckerbucks"—as some critics called them—impacted the outcome.

Zuckerberg said ahead of the election in a Facebook post that he was only trying to ensure safe voting during the pandemic for under-resourced election offices. "I agree with those who say that government should have provided these funds, not private citizens. I hope that for future elections the government provides adequate funding. But absent that funding, I think it's critical that this urgent need is met." The Center for Tech and Civic Life has argued that the grants went to 2,500 US election offices in forty-nine states to "operationalize safe and secure elections."[259]

However, it seems almost impossible Zuckerberg was unaware of the partisan bent of his donations. The Center for Tech and Civic Life mostly is funded by left-of-center donors such as the

Democracy Fund, the John S. and James L. Knight Foundation, and the Rockefeller Brothers Foundation, according to the Capital Research Center, which tracks nonprofits. The organization was founded in 2012 by Tiana Epps-Johnson, Donny Bridges, and Whitney May, all of whom previously worked together at the New Organizing Institute, which the *Washington Post* referred to as "the Democratic Party's Hogwarts of digital wizardry."[260]

For Wisconsin, Zuckerberg grants were divided almost entirely among Democrat strongholds. GOP State Assembly Speaker Robin Vos appointed former Wisconsin Supreme Court Justice Michael Gableman to be special counsel to review the 2020 election. In a 136-page interim report from the special counsel, Gableman's team said the Center for Tech and Civic Life used $8.8 million as an essentially get-out-the-vote effort in five heavily Democrat areas. The center gave Milwaukee almost $2.2 million, gave $1.3 million in Zuckerbucks to Madison election officials, and gave Green Bay election officials $1.1 million. It awarded $942,000 to Racine and another $863,000 to Kenosha.[261]

The grants turned into what the Gableman report called "a joint operation" when the CTCL and the five cities focused on increased voting in "communities of color," a presumed voting bloc for Democrats. The grant money cranked up as the cooperation increased.[262]

Cities got an extra $216,000 in Zuckerberg-financed grants to set up ballot drop boxes in "targeted neighborhoods," which, according to the special counsel's report, violated Wisconsin law. "The motive for these grants was impermissible and partisan get out the vote efforts," the report says.[263]

Moreover, the special counsel's office asserted that the election in the five jurisdictions might have violated the law "by not treating all voters the same in the same election...a bedrock principle of election law." The election officials "crossed the line between election administration and campaigning, and that never should have happened," the report says.[264]

"The Zuckerberg-funded CTCL/ Zuckerberg 5 scheme would prove to be an effective way to accomplish the partisan effort to 'turnout' their desired voters and it was done with the active support of the very people and the governmental institution [Wisconsin Election Commission] that were supposed to be guarding the Wisconsin elections administrative process from the partisan activities they facilitated," the Gableman report says.[265]

For his part, Democratic Gov. Tony Evers called the investigation a "circus" and an "embarrassment for our state." But why wouldn't he? [266]

Notably, the investigation took a turn for the worse by mid-2022 when Gableman had to face off with liberal watchdog group American Oversight in a public records lawsuit. The special counsel says his office gave hundreds of pages of documents to the group—everything requested—but admitted to deleting "irrelevant or useless" documents. A Wisconsin judge found him in contempt of court. [267]

Of the Zuckerberg money, about $5 million went to Arizona, but more than half of the money—$2.9 million—went to Maricopa County, the state's largest jurisdiction and the fourth-most populous US county, according to data from the Foundation for Government Accountability, a conservative-leaning watchdog group.[268]

In Arizona, Biden won with 49.4 percent to Trump's 49.1 percent. In four of the Biden-carried counties that received the grants, the number of Democratic voters increased by 36 percent or more, according to the foundation's data.

Maricopa County narrowly went for Trump in 2016 over Hillary Clinton. But in 2020, Biden won the county after Maricopa County had an increase of 48 percent in Democrat turnout, from 702,907 in 2016 to 1.04 million in 2020. In the Democratic-leaning Santa Cruz County, which didn't get the funding, Biden had only a 12 percent increase in turnout by Democrats.[269]

The FGA report contends: "This nearly 90,000-vote difference cannot be explained by registration increases. While Democratic voter registration in Maricopa County has grown more than Republican registration since the 2016 election, the net increase was fewer than 50,000 votes and registered Republicans still outnumber registered Democrats by more than 100,000 voters. In counties that went for Biden in 2020, Zuckerbucks seem to have helped boost Democratic turnout."[270]

While Democrat-leaning counties in Pennsylvania got 92 percent of the Zuckerberg grants, the FGA measured the allocation to counties on a per-voter basis, since urban and Democrat-leaning jurisdictions generally are more densely populated than rural, more Republican jurisdictions. In Pennsylvania, which got $20 million from the CTCL for twenty-three election jurisdictions, the FGA found that Biden-carried counties got $4.99 per registered voter compared to $1.12 per registered voter in Trump-carried counties. So, the Democrat tilt doesn't indicate that grants were scaled to population, the FGA contends.[271]

The CTCL gave about $29 million in grants to Georgia counties for the 2020 election and gave an even higher amount, a rate of $7.13 per registered voter, to Biden-carried counties compared to averaging $1.91 per registered voter to Trump-carried counties. The counties getting the most in the lead-up to the presidential election were Fulton, Cobb, and DeKalb. About half of the counties that Biden carried got Zuckerberg money, while just one-fifth of counties Trump carried received any of the Zuckerberg grants. The share of the Democratic vote increased in most Georgia counties from 2016 to 2020 by about one percentage point. However, counties that didn't get Zuckerberg-funded grants "barely budged at all," according to the FGA analysis.[272]

Zuckerberg played a big—possibly definitive—role in the 2020 election. He's certainly not the only billionaire using a vast fortune to move the rules of the election game in favor of the Left, as you will read more about in a later chapter about those bankrolling the voter suppression hysteria industrial complex.

Most Secure?

Taking the Zuckerberg money out of the equation, the Wisconsin Legislative Audit Bureau, a nonpartisan panel, identified thirty problems with the state's 2020 election administration in a fall 2021 report. The problems include inconsistent standards, unlawful orders, and uneven election law enforcement.[273]

Still, you wouldn't think such problems could exist if you only listen to some quarters.

Former Department of Homeland Security official Christopher Krebs, who ran the Cybersecurity and Infrastructure Security Agency, called the 2020 vote "the most secure in American history." He was referring to a vote that was safe from being hacked. This prompted Trump to fire him, after which Krebs told *60 Minutes*, "There was no indication or evidence that there was any sort of hacking or compromise of election systems on, before or after November 3."[274]

About a year later, federal prosecutors in New York unsealed an indictment that charged two Iranians with hacking the New York state computer election system, stealing voter registration data with the intent to carry out a cyber-intimidation campaign against Republican members of Congress and Trump campaign officials, as well as Democrat voters in the November 2020 election.[275] Now, in the absence of this hacking, Trump would have obviously still lost New York in a resounding fashion. But it does indicate some things got past Krebs. Either that or, like many government bureaucrats, he's likely to always argue his agency had a near-perfect outcome.

New York didn't matter in the grand scheme of things, but Arizona assuredly did.

Arizona Attorney General Mark Brnovich's office issued an interim report in April 2022 on its investigation of Maricopa County that found "serious vulnerabilities that must be addressed and raises questions about the 2020 election in Arizona." Brnovich, in a twelve-page letter to Arizona state Senate President

Karen Fann, said the investigation did not find large-scale fraud but said there were "instances of election fraud by individuals who have been or will be prosecuted for various election crimes." The report further said, "It is possible that somewhere between 100,000 and 200,000 ballots were transported without a proper chain of custody."[276]

In January 2022, the Maricopa County Elections Department turned over thirty-eight cases of potential voter fraud to the attorney general's office, including cases of people voting in more than one county and others voting twice in Maricopa County. However, the local elected Republican leaders of Maricopa County, who have been at odds with the state Republicans regarding the 2020 election, didn't take kindly to the report. "The bottom line: the AG has not identified even a single instance where a ballot was accepted with a non-matching signature (or signature that was later cured)," said Maricopa County Board of Supervisors Chairman Bill Gates and Maricopa County Recorder Stephen Richer in a joint statement.[277]

Before the attorney general's review, the Senate launched a controversial forensic audit done by the firm Cyber Ninjas, which found problems but affirmed Biden's win in the county—actually showing he might have had ninety-nine more votes.

In late summer 2021, Georgia Secretary of State Brad Raffensperger (recall, is no undying ally to Trump) launched a probe of the DeKalb County handling of drop box ballots in 2020 after reports about problems with the chain of custody.[278] Georgia also reported multiple examples of irregularities and mismanagement out of Fulton County, the state's largest voting jurisdiction, during the vote counting in November 2020. A state-appointed independent monitor reported sloppy practices and poor management, however, saw no evidence of "any dishonesty, fraud or intentional malfeasance."[279]

The Michigan attorney general's office, working with the Michigan secretary of state's office, secured criminal charges[280] against three women in voter fraud schemes—two of whom cast dozens of ballots for unbeknownst nursing home patients.[281]

No. This doesn't prove the 2020 outcome was illegitimate. Based on *adjudicated cases*, there is not sufficient proof that vote tallies would change enough to flip the result of three or four states needed to alter the Electoral College math. Thus, short of absolute proof, we shouldn't presume an American president is illegitimate. We also can't say either way if the outcome would be affected if the questionable procedures were not in place. Overturning elections isn't the point. The point is that the 2020 election was a mess in so many ways. If COVID-19 was a valid excuse, it doesn't explain why the Left wants to maintain those emergency COVID-19 measures for future non-pandemic elections such as mass mail-in voting, normalizing ballot harvesting, and proliferation of ballot drop boxes. The modern machine took full advantage of a pandemic to impose election rules they have long wanted to impose. Going forward, Democrats thought they could overhaul elections in their favor. With many deep-pocketed special interests backing them up, they will try to do so again.

Chapter 7

Legalizing Fraud through "Voting Rights" Legislation

Voter fraud is no longer systemic because there are basic safeguards in place to stop it from being systemic. However, the party of Tammany Hall and Jim Crow is pushing a legislative agenda to make it easier to steal elections. If enacted, such legislation would eliminate safeguards and reestablish the old school machine at a national level. Fraud and corruption would not only be systemic. It would almost be legal or at least virtually impossible to prosecute.

The proposed federal power grabs would eliminate state voter ID laws, allow Election Day registration, expand ballot harvesting, restrict cleaning the voter rolls, and establish universal mail-in voting that would, in time, eliminate in-person voting. This is really saying the quiet part out loud regardless of how benignly titled some of the bills are. These are ideas that would clearly make it easy to steal elections—only with the force of law behind them.

The top agenda item for President Joe Biden, Speaker Nancy Pelosi, and Senate Majority Leader Chuck Schumer has been the HR 1 bill that passed the House but died from a Senate filibuster.

A nominally more modest bill called the "Freedom to Vote Act" also died after being unable to gain a supermajority in the Senate. Yet another proposal, the John Lewis Voting Rights Advancement Act, named for civil rights icon John Lewis, would grant veto power to the federal government over state election laws and was passed by the House but died in the Senate. The bills are part of an agenda to ensure Democrats never lose another election by hook or by crook.

These legislative proposals turn the recommendations of the aforementioned Carter-Baker Commission on their head. The bipartisan commission supported voter ID and warned about the vulnerabilities of absentee voting. HR 1 would eliminate most voter ID laws and vastly expand mail-in voting.

The desired result is to attain a perpetual majority. It's likely Democrats are mistaken on this front. Whether it's voting laws or gerrymandering, political parties have frequently thought they found a way to gain a permanent majority only to find their opponents adapt. But, as explained earlier, Democrats historically benefit more from voter fraud than Republicans.

Corrupt Politicians Act

HR 1 is an omnibus bill—a Green New Deal of election bills—that puts much of the Democratic Party's platform into a single piece of legislation using elections as a rationale. Democrats dubbed the bill the "For the People Act." Republicans call the bill the "Corrupt Politicians Act." This is not a new proposal; the only thing that changes is the rationale. While the Green New Deal's climate rationale for expanding the entitlement state is largely nonsensical, it has been at least consistent. The rationale for passing the Democrats' election power grab keeps changing.

It was initially introduced in 2019 with a new Democrat House majority. In 2019, the legislation was supposed to prevent future Russian meddling in political campaigns. That made little sense since this didn't really address foreign interference, though it does have election security provisions such as paper ballots. The *New York Times* and other Democrat-friendly media outlets called this anti-corruption legislation. This later evolved into calling it voting rights legislation. Spoiler alert, it's neither.

House Democrats brought the same legislation up again in 2020. This time, the rationale was the COVID-19 pandemic. Voting rights had to be expanded because the health concerns made it too difficult to vote, the argument went. The legislation didn't pass, but as explained in the previous chapter, some states took some sketchy actions that year.

In 2021 the rationale became preventing another January 6 attack on democracy. It also became about stopping the "voter suppression" legislation at the state level. Same bill, but every year the public rationale was different.

A clear observation of what this legislation does—and what similar bills would do—tells a different story from a benevolent effort to save democracy.

The biggest lies about the HR 1 proposal come in a House Democrats' "fact sheet" about the proposal that claims the bill would "improve access," "promote integrity," and "ensure security."[282]

In a twenty-six-page section-by-section summary of the massive legislation, Democrats have generally said what they want to do in the 791-page bill but put the most benevolent spin on things.[283]

The inescapable fact is that this HR 1 legislation—and similar bills—would ring in a new era of machine politics that would make Tammany Hall, Richard Daley, and the Pendergast clan very proud.

Here we look at the spin vs. the truth on the most audacious election power grab attempt.

Spin: HR 1 requires states to allow voters to sign sworn affidavits in lieu of presenting photo ID.

Truth: Widely popular voter ID laws enacted in thirty-five states would be effectively banned if HR 1 was enacted. The legislation includes a mandate for states, "Permitting use of sworn written statement to meet identification requirements for voting." So every state would have to allow someone who didn't have ID to sign a sworn statement. While that's not an express ban, it would all but eliminate any teeth for voters showing they are who they say they are. If someone was voting under a different name, in the wrong precinct, or trying to vote more than once, it's not likely he or she would think twice about fibbing on a sworn statement. Also, there would be no point in bringing ID if a voter simply had to sign a statement. Moreover, ID is verifiable on the spot. A sworn statement seems to expect election officials to engage in elaborate perjury investigations if they suspect something isn't correct. The HR 1 language itself talks about "excessively onerous voter ID requirements" in states. The legislation also states, "A State may not require an individual to provide any form of identification as a condition of obtaining an absentee ballot."

Spin: The bill's provision for automatic voter registration preserves voting rights by preventing restrictive voter registration practices.

Truth: Under HR 1 and later the Freedom to Vote Act, any individual on a database for a driver's license, welfare, or just tax records would be automatically registered to vote. Requiring every state to do this would be a bureaucratic nightmare and would almost certainly lead to ineligible voters and duplicative registrants. Particularly troublesome here is that the legislation requires states automatically register all individuals and makes no mention of citizens.[284] It's little wonder why Democrats don't want to protect the border.

It shouldn't be too much for the public to expect that only legal citizens should be able to vote. Thus, requiring proof of citizenship to register to vote should be a given and is a far cry from suppression. Election offices can easily verify this through state and public databases such as the Social Security Administration, the Department of Homeland Security, and its E-Verify system.[285]

Spin: The legislation requires states to permit voters to register on the day of a federal election, including during early voting. This protects voting rights and inhibits restrictive voting practices.

Truth: This mandates every state allow Election Day registration. If someone registers minutes before voting, it is very difficult for election officials to verify their identity—particularly after ditching ID requirements—or that the person really lives at the address they are providing.

Spin: The bill will prevent voter "purges."

Truth: The legislation and even the summary assert that "failure to vote is not grounds for removing registered voters from the rolls." For one, people aren't removed simply for "failure to vote." There is a process. If voters are inactive in at least two consecutive federal elections and fail to respond to multiple notices by mail, states can remove them from the voter rolls. These voters can re-register, or if a mistake occurred, can cast a provisional ballot. The Supreme Court upheld the authority of states to do this. Lest you think this is entirely about ensuring voters aren't mistakenly removed, well, the legislation explicitly limits the authority of states to remove voters from the list based on interstate cross-checks. This means voters known to be registered in two locations could not be removed from either voter list if HR 1 were enacted.

Spin: The legislation "prohibits a state from imposing restrictions on an individual's ability to vote by mail."

Truth: HR 1 would mandate states have what the bill calls "no-fault" absentee voting. This would be universal mail-in voting. This would likely be a disaster, based on the findings of the Carter-Baker Commission. Under this plan, ballot applications (or in some states just ballots) would be mailed out to all residences. This provides opportunities to forge ballots or vote in the name of a former resident of the address.[286]

Absentee ballots are, by nature, outside the supervision of election officials and poll watchers. As explained in the ballot harvesting chapter, these ballots are more subject to fraud and intimidation, being stolen, or being forged or altered. This is not hypothetical. This is based on what has happened. The original intent for absentee voting was for people who are sick and disabled who can't make it to the polls, or for either military or those who will be out of town on Election Day. No-fault absentee voting creates too much opportunity for mischief. [287]

Spin: HR 1 "permits a voter to designate any person to return" a ballot. States should not put "any limit" on how many ballots a person can collect.

Truth: HR 1 requires states to allow vote trafficking—also known as ballot harvesting—meaning candidates, campaign staffers, or political operatives can collect the ballots.[288] As previously explained, HR 1 would also ban witness signature requirements for absentee ballots. The bill, if enacted, would also require states to allow third parties—including campaign staffers and political consultants—to pick up and deliver absentee ballots. Vote trafficking is illegal in many states, including North Carolina, where a Republican's congressional victory was overturned because of the fraud. That fraud almost certainly would have never been caught if HR 1 was the law of the land.

Spin: Election officials should not be allowed to reject a voter registration application.

Truth: The HR 1 legislation would make it a criminal offense for an election official to reject a voter registration application, even if the official believes the individual is ineligible to vote. Even if a voter cast ballots outside their precincts, states would still have to count them under this law. This would particularly be problematic for local elections. This provision would preclude election officials from using the US Postal Service's national change of address system to verify the address of registered voters or participating in an interstate program that compares voter registration lists. It also prohibits removing voters from a list who haven't voted or responded to notifications.[289]

When HR 1 crashed, the next run was the Freedom to Vote Act, or S 2747, sponsored by Sen. Amy Klobuchar, D-MN. This bill was a watered-down version of HR 1, attempting to draw more moderate support. It left voter ID laws alone, but it still required universal mail-in voting and automatic voter registration, and mandated that states allow Election Day registration. This also failed, so Democrats turned to the John Lewis Voting Rights Advancement Act, or HR 4.

Bureaucratic Veto Power

While HR 4 is not as sweeping as HR 1, it's certainly sneakier and would empower partisan bureaucrats in the Justice Department at a dangerous level to control elections. Under this proposal, the Justice Department would have veto power over state election laws such as voter ID. [290]

Spin: The proposal would simply maintain and strengthen the Voting Rights Act to what it was before the awful *Shelby County* decision by restoring preclearance.

Truth: The HR 4 bill has a "practice-based preclearance" policy that wasn't part of the 1965 Voting Rights Act before the *Shelby County* ruling. Instead of covering nine states, this would extend to every jurisdiction nationally. So, states that have not had a history of discrimination would have to get federal approval for any new "law, regulation, or policy" that adds "elected at-large" seats where two or more racial/language minority groups represent 20 percent of the voting age population.[291]

The legislation further aims to overturn three high court rulings—or at least codify into federal law what the high court ruled against. The key case the law would target is the 2013 *Shelby County v. Holder* case on preclearance. The second is the *Brnovich v. Democratic National Committee* case of 2021 that allows states to ban ballot harvesting and require voters to cast ballots in their precincts. The third is the lesser-known *Bartlett v.*

Strickland from 2009, which set parameters for redistricting and what might be considered vote dilution.

In the *Shelby County v. Holder* case, the high court found the 1965 coverage formula used in Section 5 of the Voting Rights Act was no longer applicable. It was based on low voter registration and turnout in presidential elections. The court determined the 2006 renewal of Section 5 for another twenty-five years was based on a standard not applicable to modern times based on voter registration numbers since Census Bureau data shows African American registration is on a par and at least percentagewise often exceeds white turnout in the nine states covered.

Notably untouched by the *Shelby County* decision was Section 3 of the Voting Rights Act that allows a court to impose a preclearance requirement on a jurisdiction if intentional misconduct was found that violates the Fourteenth and Fifteenth Amendments.[292] The Shelby County ruling also did not touch Section 2 that is a nationwide ban on voting practices that "result in a denial or abridgement of the right of any citizen of the United States to vote on account of race or color" or membership in a language minority group.

The *Brnovich v. Democratic National Committee* case was about proper application of Section 2 of the VRA. A court considers the "totality of the circumstances" for each case. The high court has explained that Section 2 cases "demands proof that 'the political processes leading to nomination or election in the State or political subdivision are not equally open to participation' by members of a protected class 'in that its members have less opportunity than other members of the electorate to participate in the political process and to elect representatives of their choice.'" The court found in the Arizona case that Arizona law "generally makes it very easy to vote," even with the law that wouldn't count ballots cast outside a voter's assigned precinct and the anti-vote trafficking law. The Supreme Court upheld both as falling within "certain guideposts" of Section 2 of the VRA.[293]

In the lesser-known case of *Bartlett v. Strickland*, the Supreme Court determined how to apply the law on vote dilution under Section 2 for redistricting. The court found a claim must be "sufficiently large and geographically compact to constitute a majority in a single-member district." So, that means if the allegedly discriminatory district were redrawn, the minority group making the challenge would be a majority in the new district and could have the opportunity to elect more candidates. In the *Bartlett* decision, the Supreme Court rejected the plaintiff claim that Section 2 protected a North Carolina state House district that had an African American population of 39 percent. In this case, there was not sufficient proof the votes were being diluted. The Supreme Court said it was "contrary to the mandate" of Section 2 that requires showing that minority voters "have less opportunity than other members of the electorate to…elect their candidates of choice."

These three Supreme Court rulings gave states more leeway in adopting election laws, but national legislation could seize that authority. If HR 4 were enacted, essentially any state or local election law that goes beyond the federal law would face preclearance from the federal government.

The HR 4 bill prohibits states from using real election results as evidence that minority voters weren't harmed by election laws. The math tells us that a case could easily be made in court that voter ID laws have no impact on minority voter turnout. But a state wouldn't have the chance to make that case. HR 4 turns due process on its head. If a state can't prove a law has zero impact, it must scrap it.[294]

Spin: HR 4 says it is not a defense to change election laws meant to stop "potential criminal activity" unless the stated crimes happened in "substantial numbers."[295]

Truth: This is using no-rampant fraud as an excuse to allow some fraud. It would further open states up to likely meritless litigation from various left-wing advocacy groups—thus states would very likely stop enacting election integrity laws to meet the threats to ballots.[296] HR 4 adds a provision to void voter ID laws and citizenship verification and ditch the "guideposts" the Supreme Court provided in the 2021 *Brnovich* ruling. That would make it impossible to defend voter ID laws or other election security measures.

Spin: HR 4 would require the Justice Department to find fifteen voting rights violations occurring over the past twenty-five years before it could place a state under Section 5 preclearance for ten years.

Truth: That might sound reasonable on the surface since fifteen violations is a lot. But this would apply to any local jurisdiction inside a state, even if the state and most of the local governments were not violating any voting rights. And given the Left's bastardized definition of suppression, one can assume eager Justice Department bureaucrats could be creative in how they define a voting rights violation. A political subdivision in a state—generally counties—could be placed under a preclearance requirement for three violations over twenty-five years. Importantly, a "voting rights violation" isn't just a court finding but could also include settlement agreements or consent decrees and a finding of a statistical disparity, also known as disparate impact.[297]

For now, these legislative efforts fizzled from the Senate filibuster, though the Left will continue their assault on elections with machine-oriented legislation if they manage to win bigger majorities in Congress. Until that day, the Biden administration isn't waiting around and is trying to use the administrative state as effectively as possible to acquire a permanent Democrat majority.

Chapter 8

Biden's Administrative State Election Power Grab

American democracy dodged a bullet when the Left's massive attempt at an election takeover died in Congress. But President Joe Biden and the federal bureaucracy can still find clever ways to put their thumb on the scale of elections for a favored outcome.

The last Democratic president, Barack Obama, liked to boast he had a "pen and a phone," so Congress wasn't that necessary. Biden is working with a federal bureaucracy that has the mentality that some in the FBI and intelligence agencies had in the 2016 election, feeling the ends justified the means to stop Donald Trump's election, or the rationale of some Democratic National Committee staffers who felt justified taking sides in the party primary to stop Bernie Sanders.

In this case, Biden has taken the road map for election executive action from one of the most far-left and well-funded organizations in the United States, one that has significant sway inside the Biden White House.

After the last of the Democrats' bills for a federal takeover of elections crashed and burned, Vice President Kamala Harris was on CBS News talking with Gayle King about what the next move could be.

Harris said they haven't given up on trying to pass something through Congress, but for now, the Biden administration would rely on executive actions.

"What we will do is keep fighting to get the legislation passed because that is critical. So, we are not giving up on that," Harris told King. "And then it is a matter of continuing to do the work of executive orders, doing the work through the Department of Justice, which has been litigating these cases in the various states, because we believe they are a violation of the spirit of the Constitution of the United States."

After press inquiries, the White House clarified the vice president was referring to a March 2021 executive order from Biden that directed every federal agency to focus on voter registration in what appears to be a federally funded, all-of-government get-out-the-vote effort.

Don't worry. We are assured this will be nonpartisan.

The White House came back in September 2021 to explain federal agencies will be working with private actors to increase voter participation and registration. But the Biden administration hasn't given many details about how this order is being implemented. What's key is that the executive order almost mirrors exactly what the left-wing group Demos produced in a policy brief shortly after Biden was elected, calling for the new president-elect to take executive action on election issues.

Root of "Demagogue"

Demos should be credited as among the most brazen organizations. While other groups on the left often attempt to sound reasonable and pragmatic, Demos shows ideological leg with phrases like, "transforming America," "rethinking capitalism," and "global governance."

So the group's "Democracy Program" strikes one of its least-threatening tones. Don't be fooled. It's about weaponizing the federal government to sign up as many Democrat voters as possible. Demos was highly critical of the Obama administration, claiming it did not go far enough to turn federal agencies into get-out-the-vote campaigns for the Left.

There is no need for such criticism of the Biden administration, which has seemingly implemented the entire election agenda of the New York-based think tank and advocacy group.

Demos issued a report on December 3, 2020, titled, "Executive Action to Advance Democracy: What the Biden-Harris Administration and the Agencies Can Do to Build a More Inclusive Democracy."

Less than two months after taking the oath of office, Biden issued an executive order nearly identical to the Demos demands about politicizing federal agencies, while Biden's Justice Department also seemingly took up the Demos mantle.

Lest there be any doubt about the organization's influence over this administration, it's important to know that K. Sabeel Rahman was the president of Demos when the organization issued the briefing calling for Biden's executive actions. Moreover, Chiraag Bains was the Demos legal strategies director when it made the recommendations. In early 2021, Biden appointed Rahman and Bains to top-level White House advisor jobs.

So, it's no coincidence that Rahman is senior council for the Office of Management and Budget, which oversees the implementation of executive orders, as well as for the Office of Information and Regulatory Affairs, which oversees regulation. Bains is the deputy director of racial justice and equity for the Domestic Policy Council—which the executive order identifies as taking the lead on the policy. A White House press release on March 5, 2021, noted that Bains—while working at Demos, "led voting rights litigation and advocacy across the country." Two days after this press release, Biden issued the executive order.

Before working in the White House, and before working for Demos, Bains was in the Obama administration's Justice Department, where he was a member of the team that investigated and sued Ferguson, Missouri, alleging police misconduct.[298] Bains worked at Harvard Law School before working at Demos. He also was a senior fellow at the Open Society Foundations, the organization bankrolled by far-left billionaire financier George Soros.

Rahman previously worked for the Brennan Center for Justice in his portal through the world of left-wing advocacy before finally achieving a plumb government job with the power to impose policy. He was also a fellow at the Roosevelt Institute, an organization bankrolled by the Democracy Alliance, which is funded by a group of left-wing billionaires—and he regularly participated in Democracy Alliance Conferences.[299]

Those were all rungs on a ladder to becoming the president of Demos in 2018, a time when he led the organization in its war against the Trump administration's policies.[300], [301]

Rahman, as president of Demos, was a definite shaper of Democratic policies and participated in a discussion titled "Uniting Working Men and Women Behind a Democratic Agenda" during the 2019 House Democrats Issues Conference after the party recaptured the House majority.[302]

Demos began in 2000 as a coalition of several left-wing nonprofits, along with former Congressman David Skaggs, a Colorado Democrat, and Clinton administration State Department official Linda Tarr-Whelan. The group has allied itself with The Squad, as well as Sen. Elizabeth Warren, D-MA. Warren's daughter, Amelia Warren Tyagi, is a founding member and was chairwoman of the Demos board of trustees before her mother was a senator.[303]

The name Demos is an ancient Greek word meaning "people" or "the mob." It is the root of the English word "democracy" and is also the root of the word "demagogue," which might be most fitting.

The organization says it focuses on three areas: voting rights expansion, a hybrid environmentalist-left agenda it calls "pathways to ensure a diverse, expanded middle class in a new, sustainable economy," and advocacy for communitarianism and a liberal interpretation of racial equality.[304]

Two mega foundations known for backing the Left—the Tides Foundation and the Ford Foundation—each gave more than $1 million to Demos. The Bill and Melinda Gates Foundation contributed about $900,000 to Demos. The W.K. Kellogg Foundation, one of the nation's largest nonprofits that regularly funds left-leaning causes, has given almost $500,000 to Demos. Labor unions—including the United Auto Workers, the American Federation of Teachers, the American Association of State, County and Municipal Employees, and the Communications Workers of America have also contributed to the organization.[305]

Demos Democracy Program

Demos has been part of the Democracy Initiative, a coalition of liberal groups that plotted a policy agenda for President Obama's second term shortly after his re-election in 2012. *Mother Jones* reported in January 2013 that these goals included "fighting voter ID laws."[306]

The Demos Democracy Program says it wants to "strengthen democracy in the United States by reducing barriers to voter participation and encouraging civic engagement." That sounds all well and good. But the means of getting there include ending "felon disenfranchisement," as most states have some restrictions on voting rights for people with felony convictions, or at least a process for getting those voting rights restored. The program also long advocated for "same-day voter registration," which would make it difficult for election workers to validate someone's registration.[307]

Demos partnered with Project Vote, an offshoot of ACORN, and the Lawyers' Committee for Civil Rights Under Law to lobby the federal and state governments against what it calls "excessive Voter Identification requirements."[308]

The coalition wanted the Motor Voter law extended beyond registering voters at the Department of Motor Vehicle offices to include offices for welfare, Medicaid, food stamps, and other areas of public assistance where perhaps Democrat voters are more likely to be. Demos criticized the Obama administration for not using the HealthCare.gov portal to sign up for Obamacare as a voting registration site. The marriage of government with turning out the vote was entirely the core of Boss Tweed, the Daley machine, and others.

Demos and Project Vote leaders wrote a letter to President Obama and Secretary of Health and Human Services Kathleen Sebelius that said: "Providing only a voter registration link does not comply with the law and, from a practical perspective, is grossly inadequate. A link does not 'distribute' a voter registration application because it requires applicants to have access to a printer, which many applicants do not have."[309]

Even the Obama administration seemed to realize signing up voters on Healthcare.gov would have looked unseemly, particularly when it was having such a tough time handling the political fallout of the Obamacare law itself and the problematic start to the website.

On another front, Demos and its coalition partners identified Ohio as the worst offender in its failure to sign up voters on public assistance, also known as likely Democratic voters. The states of Missouri, Tennessee, Colorado, New York, North Carolina, Georgia, New Jersey, and Texas also scored badly—so the group did toss a couple of blue states and one purple state in the mix. Demos even sued Ohio, which settled in 2009, agreeing to add 246,000 low-income voters to the rolls by November 2010.[310]

"Act as Voter Registration Agencies"

In this backdrop of spending years advocating using the power of government to benefit a single party, Demos issued its December 2020 recommendations for the incoming Biden-Harris administration in what turned out to be the blueprint for Biden's election agenda.

The first of the six recommendations says, "The Biden-Harris administration can make voting more accessible by directing specified federal agencies, in their administration of federal programs, to act as voter registration agencies, including providing voter registration applications, assisting clients to complete applications, and transmitting completed applications to state authorities."[311]

In apparent response, Biden issued an overly broad executive order on March 7, 2021, ordering federal agencies to do exactly that.

"Agencies shall consider ways to expand citizens' opportunities to register to vote and to obtain information about, and participate in, the electoral process," Biden's executive order says. "The head of each agency shall evaluate ways in which the agency can, as appropriate and consistent with applicable law, promote voter registration and voter participation." It also says agencies are to "expand citizens' opportunities to register to vote and to obtain information about, and participate in, the electoral process."

The order directs agencies to focus on "distributing voter registration and vote-by-mail ballot application forms," "assisting applicants in completing voter registration and vote-by-mail ballot application forms," and "soliciting and facilitating approved, nonpartisan third-party organizations and state officials to provide voter registration services on agency premises."[312]

Let that sink in. A whole-of-government approach to registering more people to vote. This is what Demos pushed the Obamacare website to do but on steroids. Much like the suppression myth, there is no evidence Americans who are eligible to vote are having any difficulty getting registered, as more voters were registered in the 2020 election than in the previous presidential election.

Demos specifically singled out using the Indian Health Service within the Department of Health and Human Services, and the US Citizenship and Immigration Services to sign up new voters at naturalization ceremonies, using the Social Security Administration through the Supplemental Security Income and Social Security Disability Insurance programs to drive up registration. To be fair, at least a couple of agencies specifically cited might well be more likely to attract Republican-leaning voters. The Department of Defense military pay offices, as well as using the Department of Veterans Affairs, were both directly referenced in the Demos suggestions as voter registration sites.

Under Biden's executive order, the Department of Homeland Security's focus will be on voter registration "at the end of naturalization ceremonies for the hundreds of thousands of citizens naturalized each year," according to the White House summary of agency plans. Before federal elections, the Defense Department will send information to ensure that service members are able to register to vote. The Agriculture Department's Rural Housing Service will work with lenders to provide an opportunity to register for those seeking mortgages. The Department of Health and Human Services' Administration for Community Living plans to launch a "voting access hub" to connect older adults and disabled persons with voting information, tools, and resources.

"Aggressive" Justice Department Push on Voting

The second Demos recommendation for Biden's executive actions was to "strengthen Department of Justice's enforcement of and guidance on voting rights statutes" and "pursue aggressive civil and criminal enforcement of federal voting rights protections." The Demos policy brief also said that the Justice Department should crack down on "list-maintenance programs that are non-uniform or discriminatory." This is a reference to cleaning voter rolls of inactive voters.

The Justice Department seems to have obliged, filing lawsuits against the election laws in both Georgia and Texas, while also issuing election law guidance seemingly as a warning to other states. Also, Biden appointed top Justice Department officials with a long record of opposing any voter ID laws.

Biden named Vanita Gupta as the associate attorney general. She returned to the department after running the civil rights division during the Obama administration. During that run, she oversaw the 2015 lawsuit against North Carolina to attempt to block the voter ID law there. Gupta is a former CEO of the Leadership Conference on Civil and Human Rights and was previously a lawyer with the NAACP Legal Defense and Education Fund, as well as a lawyer with the ACLU.[313]

Biden also named Kristen Clarke as the assistant attorney general, who would lead the Civil Rights Division that oversees the Voting Section. In the private sector, Clarke had a long record opposing election integrity laws. She was previously the president of the Lawyers' Committee for Civil Rights Under Law. She also previously worked for the New York attorney general's office and for the NAACP Legal Defense and Education Fund.[314]

Clarke, as a private lawyer, demanded the Justice Department dismiss a case against a black politician for violating the Voting Rights Act—even though the victims were black. Also in the private sector, while working for the Lawyers' Committee, she led a lawsuit to stop the then-Georgia Secretary of State Brian Kemp from enforcing election integrity policies.[315, 316]

While she has talked a big game, in theory, about what might suppress voting, when the rubber hit the road on a bona fide open-and-shut case of voter intimidation, she made the wrong call. Clarke, while at the NAACP LDF, pushed the Justice Department to drop its case against the New Black Panther Party, the far-left group that was intimidating voters at a Pennsylvania polling place during the 2008 election. The intimidation was, in theory, going to benefit Democrats, so it didn't matter. The Obama Justice Department complied with the push.[317]

In July 2021, the Department of Justice issued guidance

on federal statutes regarding voting methods—including mail-in voting—and warnings on conducting post-election audits. Clarke declared, "Whether through litigation or the issuance of official guidance, we are using every tool in our arsenal to ensure that all eligible citizens can exercise their right to vote free from intimidation, and have their ballots counted."

In June 2021, the Justice Department sued Georgia over its voting law regarding the use of voter ID for absentee ballots. The complaint contends that provisions of the law were adopted with the purpose of denying or abridging the right to vote based on race.[318] The following November, the Justice Department filed a lawsuit against Texas over what it claimed were "restrictive voting procedures." [319]

In late May 2022, the Justice Department issued a guide to how voting laws apply to people with criminal convictions on a state-by-state basis. The Justice Department announced the guidance was in response to Biden's March 2021 executive order.[320]

The Biden executive order says, "The Attorney General shall establish procedures, consistent with applicable law, to provide educational materials related to voter registration and voting and, to the extent practicable, to facilitate voter registration, for all eligible individuals in the custody of the Federal Bureau of Prisons."

Moreover, it said the government should "provide information about voting to individuals in federal custody, facilitate voting by those who remain eligible to do so while in federal custody, and educate individuals before reentry about voting rules and voting rights in their states."

The third Demos recommendation was to provide more federal resources to the Election Assistance Commission. Under this category, Demos called for the EAC to "develop standards and best practices for mail and early voting" and to "encourage 'no-excuse' voting by mail." [321]

Along those lines, the Biden executive order says agencies

should provide ways to give information to people from government offices located throughout the United States as well as online and social media, "about how to register to vote, how to request a vote-by-mail ballot, and how to cast a ballot in upcoming elections," and "ways to provide access to voter registration services and vote-by-mail ballot applications" and "distributing voter registration and vote-by-mail ballot application forms."[322]

Inside the White House

The fourth Demos recommendation was: "Create an office within the White House focused on advancing the administration's efforts to protect and strengthen democratic systems and civic participation. The office would coordinate across the federal government, and with state and local governments, to identify opportunities to increase civic participation among the American people through executive authority, legislation, budgets, strategic communications, and community partnerships."[323]

Sure enough, in April 2021, Biden named Justin Levitt as his senior policy advisor for democracy and voting rights. Levitt is a Loyola law professor who worked in the Justice Department's Civil Rights Division during the Obama administration.[324] Levitt was formerly on the campaign staff of retired General Wesley Clark's 2004 bid for the Democratic Party presidential nomination. After that, he went to work for the liberal political action committee America Coming Together funded by George Soros and other Democratic mega-donors.[325] He gained the Left's voting pedigree by working for the Brennan Center for Justice before going to work for the Democratic National Committee in 2008 as national voter protection counsel. After that, he returned to the Brennan Center.[326]

In 2014, Levitt wrote a Brennan Center report that said of the one billion votes cast in the United States since 2000, only thirty-one were instances of voter impersonation. This was his rationale for opposing voter ID laws.[327] In 2017, Levitt argued in a journal article titled "Quick and Dirty: The New Misreading of the Voting Rights Act" that those states used a simplified interpretation of the 1965 Voting Rights Act to allow subtle racial discrimination to curb access to the polls for minorities.[328]

He first went to work for Loyola in 2010 as an associate professor, but in 2015, took a two-year leave of absence from the university to work as deputy attorney general in the Civil Rights Division. At the end of the Obama administration, he returned to Loyola. But in April 2021, went to work for the Biden White House to advise the president on election law and voter access.[329]

Postal Service and Prison Gerrymandering

The fifth recommendation calls for the Biden-Harris administration to "strengthen the U.S. Postal Service's ability to deliver election mail." Some of this suggestion surrounded the pre-election postal conspiracy theories. It also called for Biden to "issue an executive order establishing a task force to review the process that led to service cutbacks and equipment removal in the summer and fall of 2020. The task force should issue findings and recommend changes to ensure decisions on mail delivery remain insulated from partisan interference and are implemented solely to serve the mission of USPS." Biden's executive order didn't jump into the US Postal Service quite yet, though it is another federal agency that would be covered in the whole-of-government approach.[330]

The sixth Demos suggestion was to end what it calls "Prison Based Gerrymandering" by requiring the Census Bureau to count federal prisoners at their last known address rather than at the prison they are incarcerated in. Demos suggested that Biden direct the Bureau of Prisons to inform the Census Bureau of the last known address. The theory behind this is that when it comes time for redistricting, prisoners are from urban areas that could add majority Democrat districts but are housed in rural areas—and thus will only add non-voting residents to expand likely Republican areas.

The president directed federal agencies to respond to the March 2021 executive order in two hundred days with plans reporting to White House Domestic Policy Adviser Susan Rice. That September, the White House released a four-page "fact sheet" providing only the most basic overview of what the agencies submitted but frequently mentioned that the federal agencies would partner with supposedly nonpartisan private organizations to sign up new voters.

Demos is legally nonpartisan, as are the bulk of nonprofit organizations. That doesn't mean non-ideological. Stacey Abrams's Fair Fight Action is also, legally speaking, nonpartisan. The problem is that the slim information the White House released doesn't indicate who the Biden bureaucracy will partner with in a get-out-the-vote effort.

Let's be clear, it would be problematic for a Republican president or for a president of any party to direct the federal bureaucracy to engage in elections. It's difficult to see how the public shouldn't suspect the party in power would want to shift things in their favor.

Election Integrity Caucus Confronts Executive Order

After some preliminary inquiries, thirty-six House Republicans who were part of the Election Integrity Caucus wrote a letter to the Office of Management and Budget Acting Director Shalanda Young pushing for more specifics. Reps. Claudia Tenney, R-NY, and Mike Garcia, R-CA, are the co-chairs of this caucus and were among the signers.

"This EO's strategy appears to enable the Biden administration to use federal government resources, funded by American taxpayers, to circumvent newly passed state election integrity laws," the caucus letter to OMB's Young says. "These laws make it easier to vote and harder to cheat. The Biden administration's ongoing efforts to federalize state-run elections will erode these important protections."

In some ways the Biden executive actions are more insidious than the federal takeover legislation. At least congressional votes happen in the sunlight. The Biden administration is putting the force of the federal government behind signing up voters for future elections but with almost no transparency.

"Our concern about President Biden's executive order is that it is an attempt to federalize our elections," Tenney told me in an interview, later adding, "My biggest concern is we have clear Tenth Amendment violations. The implementation of these policies could pose legal problems," Tenney said. That would include a law that prevents officials from engaging in political activity while on federal property known as the Hatch Act.

"We're looking at potential Hatch Act violations. We have these former political operatives now and actually even government agencies engaging in political operations to get votes out, which are reserved to the states and not to these federal operatives," Tenney said. "It really concerns me that there's a blurred line between these federal agencies and even funding agencies, and we're even funding salaries within the federal government by the taxpayers to engage in political operations like Demos and others."

The Department of Housing and Urban Development (HUD) sent guidance to executive directors of more than three thousand public housing authorities, or PHAs, managing 1.2 million housing units providing advice on "running a PHA–initiated voter registration drive." HUD encouraged the local authorities to engage in voter registration efforts that, in some cases, allow mass collection of voter registration forms by public housing officials.

In response to Biden's executive order, the Education Department, the White House summary says it will prepare "a tool kit of resources and strategies for increasing civic engagement at the elementary school, secondary school, and higher education level, helping more than 67 million students." This will be for students who are at or near voting age, and one must wonder if the public school system will nudge a potential voting base in one direction.

The White House doesn't state what private third-party organizations those federal agencies will be "soliciting and facilitating" in getting taxpayer dollars to help round up voters.

"Determining which third-party organizations will be approved, by whom, and based on what criteria is conveniently missing" from the order, the Election Integrity Caucus letter to OMB says. "We are concerned that agencies will not be prevented from selecting nominally nonpartisan organizations to carry out these services."[331]

GOP House members questioned why Biden would force federal agencies that are not supposed to have anything to do with enforcing election laws to become involved with voting. Clearly, this opens things up for political interference.

Ruthless Bureaucratic Control

Arguably it's supposition regarding what could happen because of the executive order. The same is technically true of HR 4, named for John Lewis, which would amend the Voting Rights Act and allow partisan bureaucrats in the Justice Department the ability to veto election laws. We can't know with certainty the rules wouldn't be carried out in a strictly professional, apolitical way.

But we do have history to turn to.

The partisan bent of what are supposed to be career, nonpartisan DOJ lawyers gained considerable scrutiny because of the unscrupulous tactics during the Donald Trump presidency. What has gotten considerably less attention is what the DOJ bureaucrats have done to gain more favorable election environments for Democrats—as revealed by a Department of Justice Office of Inspector General report and other investigations.

Before the *Shelby County* ruling, the Justice Department had a very checkered history of pushing a blatantly partisan agenda on the voting front. If past is prologue, this is a guidepost for what to expect from the bureaucracy under Biden's executive push and if some of the leftist proposals in Congress went into effect.

The Justice Department's Office of Inspector General issued a report in 2013 titled, "A Review of the Operations of the Voting Section of the Civil Rights Division." The report noted "relevant evidence established" that some "personnel and career Voting Section personnel disfavored non-traditional and reverse-discrimination cases." This included when victims of discrimination were white or Asian.[332]

The IG report further found that staff attorneys for the DOJ Voting Section reviewing the Georgia voter ID law in 2005 called a lawyer defending the law "a hand-picked Vichyite," implying the attorney was a Nazi sympathizer. "Witnesses told us that that [sic] the office politics at the time was such that certain members of the career staff resorted to black humor when describing working in the Voting Section, including comparing the Voting Section to Vichy-controlled France during the Nazi occupation of World War II."[333]

In 2006, DOJ Voting Section lawyers harassed colleagues who were engaged in enforcing the Voting Rights Act in the Noxubee County, Mississippi, case in which a black majority in the county government discriminated against white voters to the detriment of a black candidate in the county. Some in the voting section office called a Black intern who requested to join the team prosecuting the Mississippi case a "token." [334]

The inspector general reported that career DOJ employees published "highly offensive and potentially threatening statements" about colleagues on prominent left-leaning news websites, such as claiming one person had "Yellow Fever," an apparent anti-Asian term.[335] Another staffer admitted to the IG about being in a group that published comments about wanting to hang a noose in a colleague's office and posted online comments about wanting to "choke" other employees. [336]

The DOJ Office of the Inspector General released a separate 2013 report about the Voting Section of the Civil Rights Division chiefly hiring most lawyers from five advocacy groups—the American Civil Liberties Union, the NAACP, the Lawyers' Committee for Civil Rights Under Law, the National Council of La Raza, and the Mexican American Legal Defense and Educational Fund. That's not to say being part of an advocacy group should be a disqualifier from a career civil service job. But allowing only left-wing groups to be the farm team for overseeing American elections should raise red flags.[337]

A twenty-year veteran of the Voting Section, Maureen Riordan told the Senate Judiciary Committee in September 2021 about the partisanship she saw. Recalling the 2000 post-election controversy, she said "When the Florida recount occurred, I personally observed Voting Section staff discussing strategies to aid the DNC in Florida and receiving and sending faxes to [the] Democratic National Committee and campaign operatives."[338]

The Left has been waging this war to use assorted narratives to justify taking over elections. Even promoting a fiction, activists could rely on allies in the media, Hollywood, academia, and think tanks like the Brennan Center to push the talking points. But the notion didn't really catch fire until a smart, charismatic, and talented politician came along who could convince enough Americans to ignore facts as she incited emotion.

Chapter 9

Not a Good Sport: How Stacey Abrams Turned a Loss into an Empire

Under the pen name "Selena Montgomery," Stacey Abrams wrote eight romance novels. One of the novels is titled *Reckless*, and another is titled *Deception*. Both titles are appropriate descriptions for her rhetoric since losing the 2018 Georgia governor's race by about fifty-five thousand votes to Republican Brian Kemp and claiming she really won.[339]

Her continuous claims are reckless in undermining trust in elections and setting a standard for partisans to insist if their side doesn't win the game was rigged. It's deception because, well, she clearly lost her election. Since the Coca-Cola company is based in Georgia, we might even call the absurd claims from Abrams the Big Lie Classic.

"I did win my election," Abrams told an audience in Washington, DC, in March 2019. "I just didn't get to have the job."[340]

Abrams's clout as a party leader became clear based on so many prominent Democrats repeating her unfounded claim. Abrams gained enough status in her losing effort to prompt practically the entire Democratic Party to hop on board Georgia's version of the Big Lie.

As a presidential candidate, Vice President Kamala Harris bellowed, "Let's say this loud and clear, without voter suppression, Stacey Abrams would be the governor of Georgia."

Former President Barack Obama, twice-failed presidential candidate Hillary Clinton, and other big-name Democrats stumped for her during the 2018 campaign. She had an impressive showing for a state that hadn't elected a Democrat to statewide office in fifteen years, hadn't cast its electoral votes for a Democratic presidential nominee since 1992, and had never elected a woman or an African American to statewide office. She had incredible political talents and fundraising skills and came very close to winning—which she deserves credit for.

But she didn't win.

Hillary Clinton, who never quite accepted her 2016 election loss, made a similar claim in her post-election commentary on the Georgia election.

"We know, don't we, that candidates both black and white lost their races because they had been deprived of the votes they otherwise would have gotten," Clinton said in March 2019. "And the clearest example is from Georgia. Stacey Abrams should be governor, leading that state right now."[341]

The Left seems to have a fascination with Abrams. She even managed to deliver the opposition party's response to a State of the Union and came off looking better for it—which rarely happens for either side.

Abrams has become one of the leading faces and voices of the national Democratic Party since her 2018 loss. Although she didn't invent the voter suppression hysteria industrial complex, she has turned it into an industry like no other politician. She has never conceded her loss was legitimate, and why would she if claiming she won has made her a celebrity? After starting Fair Fight Action, she became a regular on the Democrat speaking circuit, routinely introduced—without evidence—as the rightful governor of Georgia. A glimpse of her career, campaigns, ambitions, and talent for manipulating the public tells us a lot about the new Democrat machine, the big moneyed interest behind it, and what to expect from the machine in future elections.[342]

Fair Fight Action was actually founded in 2014, initially known as the Voter Access Institute, but changed the name after Abrams's 2018 loss. With the name change, the organization also changed its bylaws that prohibited it from getting directly or indirectly involved in elections.[343]

Had Abrams won the 2018 election, she would likely be far less of a political celebrity as she juggled pesky problems such as fixing Georgia highways, funding public schools and public universities, crime prevention, balancing the state budget, and other cumbersome tasks that governors must handle. It is difficult to think of a single candidate who gained as much from losing an election.

The media is fond of calling out Donald Trump for claiming "without evidence" that the election was rigged. Abrams has been doing the same—and she lost the state of Georgia by five times as many votes as Trump lost the Peach State by in 2020. Still, she has only gotten fawning treatment from the mainstream media.

When speaking at the 2019 annual convention of Al Sharpton's National Action Network, Abrams said, "Despite the final tally and the inauguration and the situation we find ourselves in, I do have a very affirmative statement to make: We won. …Concession needs to say something is right and true and proper. You can't trick me into saying it was right."[344]

Speaking at an Annie's List fundraiser for progressive women candidates, Abrams called Kemp an "architect of voter suppression" and was quite blunt.

"If you want to run for office again you've got to concede the election so that everyone knows that you're a good sport. I am not," Abrams said.

No kidding.

In the same speech, she declared, "I'm here to tell you a secret that makes Breitbart and Tucker Carlson go crazy: We won.

I am not delusional. I know I am not the governor of Georgia—possibly yet."[345]

Debt and Fiction: A Political and Business Life

Abrams grew up in Gulfport, Mississippi, the daughter of United Methodist ministers and sister to five siblings. She earned a bachelor of arts degree at Spelman College, a master's from the LBJ School of Public Affairs at the University of Texas, and graduated from Yale Law School.

Abrams said she did not regret attending a 1992 protest, while a freshman at Spelman College, on the steps of the Georgia Capitol that included the burning of a Georgia state flag. She said the state flag was a symbol of systemic racism and the Confederacy.[346]

Outside the political realm, Abrams was an Atlanta tax attorney and founded NOW Account Network Corporation, which is a payment services system for businesses. Abrams also co-founded the beverage company Nourish, Inc.[347] NOW Account Network did get numerous state contracts during a time when Abrams was a state legislative leader—a matter that emerged in the gubernatorial campaign. However, her 16 percent share in the company fell easily within the Georgia law that requires state officials have only a 25 percent or less stake in private companies that do business with the state.[348]

This tax lawyer who made money advising others on taxes entered the governor's race after racking up a $50,000 debt to the Internal Revenue Service. She said this is because she was spending much of her money to assist her family in Mississippi who were devastated by the 2005 Hurricane Katrina.[349]

As mentioned, Abrams was a successful novelist, admitting on the "Selena Montgomery" website that: "Selena Montgomery is the nom de plume of Stacey Abrams—she is the two-time *New York Times* bestselling author of *Our Time Is Now* and *Lead from the Outside*, an entrepreneur; and a political leader. As Selena Montgomery, she is an award-winning author of eight romantic suspense novels."[350]

She began writing romance novels as a law student at Yale but continued writing well into her career in the Georgia State Legislature, even telling the *Atlanta Journal-Constitution* she based her characters off legislative colleagues.[351] Other titles are *Rules of Engagement, The Art of Desire, Power of Persuasion, Never Tell, Hidden Sins*, and *Secrets and Lies*. Lacking enough power of persuasion over the Georgia electorate in 2018, she seems to have turned to the thin Democrat majority in Congress to federalize the rules of engagement for elections nationally.

"I Cannot Concede" The Political Rise and Near Fall

Abrams was first elected to the Georgia House of Representatives in 2006, representing an Atlanta district. By 2010, she rose to become the Democratic Party leader in the Georgia House of Representatives, the first woman in the state's history to serve as a party leader.[352]

She founded the New Georgia Project, which focused on registering young and minority voters in the state. The group, which launched in 2014, registered seventy-thousand voters ahead of her campaign.[353, 354]

Her title *Secrets and Lies* might even apply to the New Georgia Project, a group accused of being secretive about its funding. State Rep. Stacey Evans, a Democratic primary opponent of Abrams in the 2018 governor's race, accused the New Georgia Project of overstating its voter registration claims when compared to federal election data that showed far fewer fully registered.[355] After a review by the Georgia Secretary of State's office, fifty-three voter registration forms were found to be forged.[356]

During her campaign for governor, Abrams seemingly

predicted that illegal immigrants would vote to help Democrats win in 2018, asserting to cheers at a rally in Jonesboro, Georgia, "But the thing of it is, the blue wave is African American. It's white, it's Latino, it's Asian Pacific Islander. It is disabled. It is differently abled. It is LGBTQ. It is law enforcement. It is veterans," Abrams said to cheers. "It is made up of those who are told they are not worthy of being here…those who are documented and undocumented."[357]

Kemp's fifty-five thousand-vote margin was a narrow victory of 50.2 percent to 48.8 percent of the vote. That's very close but still outside the margin that fraud or vote denial would typically be able to change the outcome.

Kemp's November 6, 2018, win was among the few bright spots for the Republican Party that took a beating and lost control of the US House of Representatives, though the GOP expanded the Senate majority.

It wasn't until November 16, ten days later, that Abrams told her supporters she accepted the loss as a legal matter but was not conceding: "This is not a speech of concession, because concession means to acknowledge an action is right, true, or proper. As a woman of conscience and faith, I cannot concede that." But she said her "assessment is the law currently allows no further viable remedy."

This was at least an early hint she would be on a crusade to change election laws.

Real Story of the Georgia 2018 Election

The result was controversial primarily because Brian Kemp was the Georgia secretary of state (the state's chief election official) at the same time he was running for governor. While that's not unheard of in states across the country, it's not an unreasonable concern that—as Abrams said in the updated preface to her book, *Lead from the Outside*, Kemp was "both contestant and referee." She wrote proudly about her "non-concession" speech.

"When called upon to accept the results of the vote would not give me victory, I accepted the math. But when told to perform the traditional dance of concession, I vigorously declined," Abrams wrote in the updated version of the book. "I knew that, according to the law, I had to tell my fellow Georgians that our jointly imagined future would be delayed, I refused to play my scripted part. Because the game had been rigged. Again."

Abrams may genuinely feel she was hosed in the 2018 Georgia election. But Black voter turnout reached a record in 2018 in Georgia. So, if Kemp and the state of Georgia were engaged in a nefarious voter suppression plot, they did a horrible job pulling it off. Post-election, neither Abrams nor her supporters have ponied any evidence of impropriety.

Abrams, in her book, complained poor communities were "without equipment for voting" and had to use "antiquated machines." She added that voters were "turned away because they had been illegally purged."

FiveThirtyEight reported that 55 percent of eligible Georgians voted in the 2018 midterm election. That means a 21 percent increase for the Georgia midterm average ranging from 1982 to 2014 turned out in 2018 to vote—which is rather astounding.[358]

As David French wrote in *National Review* after the 2018 election: "If Georgia's Brian Kemp is a vote suppressor, he's the least successful vote suppressor alive. Turnout in Georgia was immense. In the previous gubernatorial election, Republican Nathan Deal won with 1.3 million votes. In November, Abrams *lost* with 1.9 million votes. There were roughly 2.5 million total votes cast in 2014. In 2018, more than 3.9 million Georgians voted."[359]

As secretary of state, Kemp enforced cleaning the voter lists and Georgia's "exact match" law, which directed election officials to flag any voter registration application if the information didn't match the voter's information in existing records. This, of course, would, at worst, mean a voter would have to cast a provisional ballot.

As explained in Chapter 4, the Help America Vote Act of 2002 requires states to regularly remove duplicate and ineligible names. Overall, Georgia removed 1.5 million voters from voter registration lists, but that included people who died or moved. The state's "use it or lose it" law, which passed under a Democrat-controlled legislature and was signed by a Democrat governor, sent voters who hadn't voted in three years a mailed notice with thirty days to respond. If the voters don't respond and then don't vote for two elections, they are removed from Georgia's voter list. Also, let's note that if these voters are improperly removed, they can re-register either in person at a county office or on Georgia's online registration system. Moreover, every "pending" voter can still vote if they show up with valid voter ID.[360]

The Justice Department—before the 2013 *Shelby County* decision—gave preclearance approval to the Georgia voter ID process in 2010 that required either a driver's license number or Social Security number to verify the voter's identity. The NAACP later sued, claiming the ID law was too restrictive. So, then-Secretary of State Kemp settled the lawsuit in 2017, and a Republican-controlled legislature tweaked the law in line with the NAACP settlement, with the same principle that last name, first initial of first name, and date of birth must have an exact match with the appropriate database. Thus, the law was called an "exact match" law.[361]

Under the 2017 exact match law, if there is not a match, the form is placed on pending status, and the applicant is notified in a letter the county election board of registrars needs additional information. The would-be voters have twenty-six months from the date of the original application to clear up issues. If they don't clear it up, their application is rejected.[362] Ahead of the election, a federal judge ordered Kemp's office to reinstate three thousand voters initially deemed invalid.[363]

Defending the "pending" status of seventy-five thousand

voter registrations—of a record seven million registered that year—Kemp said that year that 9,224 of those in the pending category were minors under the age of eighteen. Another 2,935 appeared to have used a fake address. He added that 3,393 were not citizens, and 5,842 were already registered—or were duplicate registrations. Of the remaining voter registration applications, a full 75 percent submitted the wrong Social Security information. Kemp further added that about a quarter of what he called "sloppy forms" came from the Abrams-run group, New Georgia Project's registration effort.[364]

Abrams also griped that long lines are a pain on Election Day and can discourage voters from waiting it out. But Kemp didn't control the local precincts. It turned out that about 550 voting machines in Cobb County, 700 in Fulton County, and 585 in DeKalb County were sitting unused in government warehouses. That was because of a federal lawsuit brought by Democratic Party activists that claimed the machines were vulnerable to hacking or tampering. The previous December, US District Judge Amy Totenberg, an Obama appointee, ordered the machines be sequestered to preserve evidence in a lawsuit seeking to move Georgia from electronic voting machines to paper ballots.[365, 366]

Post-Election Empire

Separate from Abrams's Fair Fight Action, a 501(c)(4) group that advocates for policy, she established Fair Fight PAC, which is engaged directly in campaigns. Abrams has also been a board member for the Center for American Progress, the most prominent think tank on the left.[367]

During the Democrat rebuttal to President Trump's 2019 State of the Union address, she said: "Let's be clear, voter suppression is real. From making it harder to register and stay on the rolls to moving and closing polling places to rejecting lawful ballots, we can no longer ignore these threats to democracy."

Abrams ignored that during eight years of the Obama administration, the Justice Department brought just five cases related to Section 2 of the Voting Rights Act.

Nevertheless, facts weren't that important. Former senior Obama adviser Dan Pfeiffer tweeted after her rebuttal that "Stacey Abrams should run for President." Senate Democratic Leader Chuck Schumer of New York tried to recruit her for a Georgia Senate run thinking—correctly as it turned out—that the GOP senators were vulnerable in the 2020 election.[368]

In a contradictory statement, Abrams said on MSNBC: "I ran a race where…we tripled Latino turnout, Asian-Pacific Islander turnout, increased youth participation rates by 138 percent, increased black turnout by 40 percent, and I got the highest share of white voters in a generation. It is not a zero-sum game, and we have to remember that winning elections is about building the largest coalition possible."[369]

So, if all that's the case, where was the suppression? She is apparently arguing a negative that if not for all the diabolical tactics by Kemp, the turnout would have been even higher.

Fair Fight Action sued the state of Georgia, claiming minorities were denied the right to vote because of "discriminatory voting barriers reminiscent of the Jim Crow era." The lawsuit didn't try to reverse the outcome of the 2018 Georgia gubernatorial election but did call for the state to stop updating voter rolls and to ban touchscreen voting machines.[370, 371]

The lawsuit also accuses Kemp of using his former position as secretary of state, with oversight of state elections, to try to prevent minority voters from casting ballots. In a loss for Abrams in December 2019, the US District Court for the Northern District of Georgia ruled it would not order the state to reinstate all the voters removed from the registration rolls because of inactivity.[372]

Though she didn't win her case, Abrams's activism may

have put things in motion for many of the problems in Georgia in the 2020 election. In 2019, under pressure, the Republican-controlled legislature passed and Kemp signed a law to relax the signature requirements. That wasn't enough. The Democratic Party of Georgia, the Democratic Senatorial Campaign Committee, and the Democratic Congressional Campaign Committee sued Georgia Secretary of State Brad Raffensperger to get the state to make further changes to matching signatures on mail-in ballots. Raffensperger entered a consent decree with the Democrat plaintiffs that made it more difficult to reject mail-in ballots that seem suspicious.[373]

For more parallels of Abrams post-election infrastructure and the Trump legal team after 2020, Fair Fight Action also supported the Coalition for Good Governance that pushed conspiracy theories about Dominion Voting Systems. In the post-2020 election, Dominion filed a $1.3 billion lawsuit against several people and media outlets that made or quoted unsubstantiated claims about the company's voting machines being rigged. "Yes, @fairfightaction has been a generous contributor to our litigation. They have been the largest single contributor to date," CGG Executive Director Marilyn Marks wrote in a tweet on January 27, 2019.

"We are proud that Stacey Abrams's Fair Fight Action organization has been a generous donor to advance our efforts that benefits voters and Fair Fight's far-reaching voting rights lawsuit as well," Marks wrote in the report released on February 8, 2019. Later that year on November 14, Marks thanked Fair Fight Action for their "support" in a tweet. This coalition was among the plaintiffs that sued Georgia in 2017 demanding the use of hand-marked paper ballots for elections—leading to those hundreds of voting machines stashed away. *Curling v. Kemp* claimed Secretary of State Kemp allowed the use of an unsecure voter registration database. Fair Fight Action called for supporters to "pack the courthouse" for the CCG group in a July 2019 event. The event's flyer called Dominion voting equipment "unauditable and unconstitutional," the *Daily Wire* reported.[374]

As it turns out, being a sore loser pays with regards to expanding speaking gigs and book deals. When Abrams ran for governor in 2018, her debts were an issue, and she had a net worth of $109,000. When she ran again, according to her March 2022 financial disclosure report, she had a net worth of $3.17 million.[375]

The Biden-Abrams Connection

Though a big star and valuable surrogate for Biden in Georgia in 2020, those in the Biden campaign were dismissive of Abrams as a potential vice presidential candidate despite all the chatter. With the onset of a pandemic, Biden was trying to sell competence in a crisis. But as the oldest presidential nominee in history, having a vice president whose highest office was serving as a state legislator a heartbeat from the presidency—was a strike against her. That said, it's not even debatable that Abrams has political skills far exceeding that of Biden's eventual choice—Kamala Harris, a US senator and former California attorney general.

"Stacey isn't ready on day one. Even she knows that and it's why she's engaging in this dance," a Biden campaign insider told the *New York Post*. "She might get perfunctorily better, but she's not a serious pick for him. And her campaign is viewed as much as promotion for her book as it is for being chosen as Biden's VP."[376]

Still, Biden didn't cut ties with her or Fair Fight Action, even though he gave remarks quite counter to Abrams's outlook. After the Electoral College formally elected him as president in December 2020, Biden said the election process "should be celebrated, not attacked." Biden derided "baseless claims about the legitimacy of the results." Finally, he said, "Respecting the will of the people is at the heart of our democracy, even if we find those results hard to accept." He was, of course, talking about Donald Trump's claims. But the same would apply to Abrams.

The bizarre irony was that the Joe Biden-Kamala Harris transition team included Jose Morales, the deputy director for voter protection at Fair Fight Action. Morales was serving on the agency review team to pick Biden administration staffers for the Justice Department. The Justice Department review team was tasked with evaluating incoming staff for the department, as well as for the Federal Election Commission, and the US Election Assistance Commission, among other agencies, according to the transition team's website.

In January 2022, two years into his presidency, Biden appointed Abrams confidante Dara Lindenbaum to the Federal Election Commission. Lindenbaum represented Fair Fight Action in a late 2018 federal lawsuit against the state of Georgia, where she signed onto a complaint filled with unproven allegations, including a claim that "one troubling problem—encountered by several voters—is that voting machines switched their votes from Leader Stacey Abrams to Secretary Kemp." Asked about this claim during her May 2022 confirmation hearing in the Senate, she responded the case is in active litigation. That much is true, noted Georgia Attorney General Chris Carr. But, he added, Fair Fight Action has dropped numerous allegations from the original complaint as the lawsuit has lingered.

It is worthwhile to imagine how Democrats and the media would react if a Republican president nominated former Trump lawyers Sidney Powell, John Eastman, or Rudy Giuliani to the FEC.

"This [Lindenbaum] appointment shows the hypocrisy of the left," Carr told me in an interview. "When some Trump supporters claimed machines switched votes from Trump to Biden in 2020, Democrats went bananas. But Democrats made the same claims in 2018."

Coining "Jim Crow 2.0"

When Georgia passed Senate Bill 202, the election reform bill that added a voter ID requirement to absentee ballots, Abrams threw the most reckless rhetorical grenades, tweeting: "From passage of the #SB202 voter suppression bill targeted at Black and brown voters to the arrest of a Black legislator who was advocating for the voting rights of her constituents, today was a reminder of Georgia's dark past." She continued, "We must fight for the future of our democracy #gapol."

In another statement, she said: "Republican state leaders willfully undermine democracy by giving themselves authority to overturn results they do not like. Now, more than ever, Americans must demand federal action to protect voting rights as we continue to fight against these blatantly unconstitutional efforts that are nothing less than Jim Crow 2.0."[377]

But to demonstrate the disingenuousness of her argument, Abrams championed the New Jersey early voting law, a so-called voting rights bill, making a virtual appearance when Democratic Gov. Phil Murphy signed the law.

In her role as a Democrat national spokesperson on voting legislation, exclaimed, "I am so excited to be looking up, looking at New Jersey, knowing that New Jersey is taking us in the right direction." [378]

The "right direction" means, as mentioned earlier, nine fewer days of early voting than the seventeen days enacted under the Georgia bill she called "Jim Crow 2.0."

Abrams is back as a candidate in 2022 for governor. In one sense that's surprising. If she runs again and loses—her star power will quickly evaporate, however she could likely continue to be a national player through her interest groups. But she likely considered that stardom could not last forever as a non-office holder. And winning the Georgia governor's race would make her an instant presidential contender in either 2024 or 2028.

If she wins, she will have an even more powerful platform to speak of a rigged election system. However, it might become more difficult for her to make the case that a system that made her governor was rigged. Part of her selling point was being a victim of suppression. If she loses again, we already know what she will say.

Though, in that case, it seems few are likely to believe her when she says again the election was rigged. So, after 2022, the suppression hysteria industrial complex may need a new spokesperson regardless of how the Georgia election shakes out. It's difficult to see at this juncture whether Democrats can find another national suppression spokesperson with the political skills of Abrams.

Abrams emerged as a star for the Democrat machine, the public face that is able to provide an almost happy face to grievance and shouting unfair. Behind the scenes the voter suppression hysteria industrial complex is far more threatening, with a vast network of billionaires and dark money.

Chapter 10

Bankrolling the Suppression Hysteria Industrial Complex

Finally, it takes big money to push a big lie. As noted, Stacey Abrams turned the suppression lie into a branding gimmick. But this fearmongering industry has the ultimate goal of a reemergence of the old-school machine that keeps Democrats in power for perpetuity. That didn't start with Abrams. Just as the first incarnation of Tammany Hall relied on big money to align government and turn out the vote, so does the current aspiring national machine. It's time to reveal how the Brennan Center for Justice, various George Soros-financed organizations, and more recently the Arabella Advisors network of dark money groups have pushed an evidence-free myth into the mainstream in a campaign to stop election integrity reforms most Americans support.

For a myth to have life, it needs infrastructure. This myth has plenty of physical and human infrastructure that includes left-wing think tanks, political action committees, and other nonprofits—many of which are not required to disclose their donors. Some are single-issue groups, focused entirely on what they characterize as "voting rights." Others are multifaceted but make election or "democracy reform" a key component of their agendas.

Much like Tammany Hall, which reigned for nearly two centuries winning elections by any means necessary, today's version is nominally more subtle. Tammany Hall 2.0 vigorously works to block any legal mechanism to stop fraud. Thus, these nonprofits and Democrats that want to make fraud easier feed off one another. Concurrently, Tammany Hall 2.0 pushes legal changes at the national and state level to make cheating easier and in the case of HR 1, encourage it. Key to this is not just the politicians but also the interest groups pumping money and propaganda behind the machine—a multiheaded beast.

Among the largest donors that have contributed to multiple groups denying voter fraud and peddling voter suppression were Fidelity Investments Charitable Gift Fund, the Joyce Foundation, several Rockefeller-aligned nonprofits, the Tides Foundation, the Ford Foundation, and the Carnegie Corporation of New York.

Here's a look at the major pressure groups and the money behind them.

Brennan Center for Justice

The Brennan Center for Justice has taken the lead in pushing the narrative. In addition to major left-of-center nonprofits, major New York City law firms contribute heavily to the Brennan Center for Justice.[379]

Brennan also has its share of major corporate donors.

Fidelity Investments Charitable Gift Fund gave at least nine grants totaling $2.28 million to the Brennan Center. The Boston-based nonprofit arm of the financial firm Fidelity Investments is the largest public charity in the United States with $30 billion in assets. It is also a reoccurring funder of these groups. Because of its vast array of recipients, the organization has even come under fire from the Left for giving to conservative organizations.[380]

Another corporate donor is the Capital One Foundation, which gave $10,000 to the Brennan Center. The Melaleuca Foundation, the charitable arm of the Melaleuca wellness company, gave another $950,000 across three grants.

Most donors had no corporate ties.

Far and away, the biggest funder to Brennan has been the Kohlberg Foundation, which has given a dozen grants totaling $15.78 million, according to information compiled by the Capital Research Center, a nonprofit watchdog group in Washington. The Kohlberg Foundation was established by private equity billionaire Jerome Kohlberg in 1989 and aims dollars at left-leaning legal advocacy and environmental organizations.

The Lakeshore Foundation has given $3 million to the Brennan Center. This is an organization based in Birmingham, Alabama, that focuses primarily on health care and health policy, as well as fitness and health for disabled people.[381]

One of the Left's biggest financiers, the Tides Foundation, gave $1 million to Brennan, according to data from the Capital Research Center. The San Francisco-based Tides Foundation was founded in 1976 by political activist Drummond Pike and financed by Jane Lehman, heiress to the fortune generated by the Reynolds tobacco conglomerate. Recent financial information shows the group has more than $500 million in assets and doled out $475 million to various left-wing causes. In recent years the organization has spent its fortune on Black Lives Matter, Media Matters, Planned Parenthood, Democracy Now, the ACLU, and others.

The John and Wendy Neu Foundation issued more than a dozen grants surpassing $2 million to the Brennan Center as did the Bernard and Anne Spitzer Charitable Trust, the grantmaking organization that was established by the parents of disgraced former New York Gov. Eliot Spitzer.

The Mai Family Foundation made a dozen contributions totaling $1.8 million to the Brennan Center. This organization was established by Vincent A. Mai, a South Africa-born investment banker who became the CEO of Cranemere, LLC. He is a former employee of the leveraged buyout firm AEA Investors and past managing director of Lehman Brothers. The foundation has funded left-wing groups such as Media Matters for America and the Soros co-founded group Institute for New Economic Thinking.[382]

The Bauman Family Foundation gave eleven grants reaching a total of $1.78 million to the Brennan Center. The Bauman Family Foundation is another reoccurring donor to special interest groups that make up the modern-day machine. It also has ties to the Democracy Alliance, a collective of left-of-center donors.[383] The head of the foundation, Patricia Bauman, has given hundreds of thousands of dollars to Democrats for office.[384]

The Leland Fikes Foundation, aligned with Texas oil magnate and Democrat donor Lee Fikes, doled out twenty-one grants for a total of $1.27 million to the Brennan Center for Justice.

Another fifteen grants reaching $1.19 million came from the Mertz Gilmore Foundation, a New York-based nonprofit that focuses on environmental, immigration, and LGBTQ issues in the city.

The Chicago-based Joyce Foundation established in 1948 has been a significant donor to the special interest groups that undermine election integrity and gave a total of $1 million to the Brennan Center. It also regularly finances advocacy for gun control, left-wing education policy, and backs left-of-center nonprofit media outlets.

The Quadrivium Foundation is a left-wing grantmaking institute associated with James and Kathryn Murdoch, notably left-leaning members of the family of Rupert Murdoch. The organization has also been engaged in fighting cybercrime and cyber-bullying.[385] It gave $1 million to the Brennan Center.

The Proteus Fund, a liberal donor-advised fund provider, gave ten grants to Brennan reaching $967,000. Established in 1995, the fund routed hundreds of millions of dollars from major left-wing donors or grantmaking organizations to activist groups on the left that have pushed for such causes as same-sex marriage, abolishing the death penalty, and cutting military spending.[386]

The Vital Projects Fund, a left-leaning grant maker fund, reached $900,000 after ten grants to the Brennan Center. The Vital Projects Fund has supported liberal initiatives on criminal justice reforms and has donated to the American Civil Liberties Union and the Netroots Foundation.

The Overbrook Foundation, a New York nonprofit established in 1948 that largely focuses on environmental and LGBTQ causes, contributed $725,000 to the Brennan Center.

The Margaret and Daniel Loeb Family Third Point Foundation, a New York-based nonprofit founded in 2000 that pushes LGBT rights, criminal justice reform, education, and Alzheimer's research, gave $710,000 to the Brennan Center.[387]

The Public Welfare Foundation, a left-wing grantmaking group founded in 1947 that focuses on criminal justice reform and boosting union-based employment, gave $660,000 to the Brennan Center.

The Marty and Dorothy Silverman Foundation, which regularly funded apolitical causes for veterans, Jewish causes, and hospitals, gave $605,000 to the Brennan Center. The organization has also been a donor to Planned Parenthood, the nation's largest abortion provider; the far-left interest group, People for the American Way; and liberal government watchdog group Citizens for Responsibility and Ethics in Washington.[388]

The Craig Newmark Foundation, named for the founder of Craig's List, contributed $550,000 to the Brennan Center, as did the Wallace Global Fund, run by the family of former left-wing Vice President Henry Wallace, and the Colorado-based Bohemian Foundation, with ties to the liberal Democracy Alliance.

The Chicago-based Howard and Jackie Shapiro Foundation, which has given to multiple philanthropies including environmental causes, contributed $527,000 to the Brennan Center.[389] The New Jersey-based L.R. Bauman Foundation, which broadly focuses on charitable organizations, was established in 2014 and gave $500,000 to the Brennan Center.

Higher profile donors gave less—but still significant amounts of money to the organization. The Jennifer and Jonathan Allan Soros Foundation gave three grants valued at $250,000 to the Brennan Center. As you might have guessed, Jonathan Soros is the son of left-wing billionaire George Soros. This foundation gave to other left-wing donor groups such as the Arabella network's New Venture Fund, the Tides Foundation, and Fidelity Investments Charitable Trust.

The Rockefeller Family Fund, reoccurring donors, gave four grants to the Brennan Center totaling $231,000. Despite the lineage, the Rockefeller Family Fund has advocated for oil divestment and funded far-left environmental group Greenpeace. It has contributed to the Ralph Nader-founded lobbying group, Public Citizen, and to the Working Families Party that fields far-left third-party candidates or endorses Democrats in state elections.[390]

The Ford Foundation—a typical donor to the left-wing causes and reoccurring funder to the suppression hysteria complex—gave $160,000 to the Brennan Center. Once the largest foundation in the United States, the Ford Foundation has lapsed behind other nonprofits but remains a powerful funder of progressive causes. One of its biggest initiatives has been trying to fund social change through courts by funding such organizations as the Environmental Defense Fund, the Mexican American Legal Defense and Education Fund, and pushing an agenda for law schools.[391]

The Streisand Foundation, named for far-left entertainer Barbara Streisand, gave $81,500. The foundation has also donated to Planned Parenthood, Media Matters, the Feminist Majority, and other groups on the left.

Ralph Nader's Public Citizen Foundation gave $15,500 to the Brennan Center.

Private donors and foundations are free to donate to whomever they wish. But the Brennan Center regularly characterizes itself as nonpartisan. The source money behind it suggests otherwise.

Fair Fight

Stacey Abrams founded her Fair Fight empire based entirely on her claim of getting robbed in the 2018 election. A mix of corporate money and far-left groups have financed her lobbying arm known as Fair Fight Action and her political arm, Fair Fight PAC.

The Fair Fight Political Action Committee is a legally separate organization that raises and spends money for political campaigns, supporting candidates it claims will oppose voter suppression. Abrams and the Georgia Democratic Party founded the Fair Fight PAC, which focused on twenty different states for the 2020 election to fund "robust voter protection operations." It also created the Legislative Victory Fund that spent heavily on Georgia state legislative races.[392]

Donors to the Fair Fight PAC include former New York Mayor Michael Bloomberg, who contributed $5 million in October 2019, clearly a time when he wanted to curry favor for his late entry into the Democratic presidential primary field for 2020.[393]

Big labor also did its part to back Fair Fight PAC. The United Auto Workers, Communications Workers of America, the National Education Association, and AFSCME each contributed $1 million during the 2020 election cycle. The AFL-CIO contributed $500,000 to Fair Fight PAC.[394]

Stacy Schusterman, former Samson Energy CEO and head of another group called the Freedom to Vote Alliance that popped up in 2022, gave $495,000 to Fair Fight PAC in 2020.[395]

Among the largest donors to the Fair Fight PAC is California progressive activist Karla Jurvetson, who gave about $1 million. Massachusetts Sen. Elizabeth Warren—who has verbally bought into the Abrams Big Lie about the 2018 election—gave the group $10,000.[396]

Fair Fight Action's biggest donor by far is Fair Fight PAC, which has given $16.3 million.

The group Defeat by Tweet contributed $192,381 to Fair Fight Action. Other donors, such as the Sheet Metal, Air, Rail and

Transportation Union gave $45,000 and the Women's Political Committee contributed $35,000 to Fair Fight Action.[397]

Incite Labs gave $100,000 to Fair Fight Action in 2019. The liberal nonprofit makes election reform one of its key priorities. Along with Fair Fight Action, it lists as its partners the Florida Rights Restoration Coalition (FRRC) that advocates for restoring the rights of felons to vote; to a group known as Co-Equal, which provides staffing and resources to Democrats involved in congressional investigations; and Win the Era, a group that endorses down ballot candidates to create a "pipeline" for future high-profile candidates.[398]

The Tides Foundation, a left-wing bankroller for multiple groups, gave $50,000 to Fair Fight Action.

The Glustrom Family Foundation, a relatively new Georgia-based charitable group, gave Fair Fight Action $50,000 in 2019.

The Silicon Valley Community Foundation gave $40,000 to Fair Fight Action. The group is a left-wing grant maker with more than $11 billion in assets. Created in 2006, the Mountain View, California-based nonprofit geared much of its spending toward the ACLU, the Drug Policy Alliance that pushes for lenient laws on drugs, the Sierra Club environmental group, and Planned Parenthood, as well as the Center for Tech and Civic Life, which played a pivotal role in the 2020 election by sending the Mark Zuckerberg-funded grants to Democrat strongholds.

On average, Abrams's Fair Fight empire didn't quite draw the same volume of high dollar contributions as the Brennan Center, but the group is gradually catching up, as Abrams became the public face of the machine's favorite myth.

Arabella Advisors Network

The way Arabella Advisor's network of nonprofits is structured makes it difficult to say how many fiscally-sponsored groups it has, how many are focused on voting issues, and how much money is flying out on this issue of voting and elections. Arabella Advisors is a private, for-profit public relations firm that runs four key nonprofits. The Sixteen Thirty Fund is a lobbying organization, or 501(c)(4) under the tax code. The New Venture Fund is the education arm, or 501(c)(3). The Hopewell Fund and the Windward Fund are also 501(c)(3) education and research groups in the network that are not quite as active as Sixteen Thirty and NVF.

These groups fiscally sponsor a vast array of organizations that in some cases spin off to become an independent nonprofit, or in other cases are simply pop-up groups or front organizations that emerge in a congressional district or state for a single campaign cycle or during a single policy debate. These pop-up groups rarely have any discernable staff, just a website, and still spend millions on issue advocacy. Front groups fiscally sponsored by Arabella organizations don't have to legally incorporate with the Internal Revenue Service since they are part of an existing 501(c)(3) or 501(c)(4).

The Arabella Advisors Network raised $1.7 billion in 2020 alone to spend toward the defeat of President Donald Trump, easily the largest amount in any year for an organization that has raised $4.7 billion since it began the dark money network in 2006.[399]

The Capital Research Center first reported on a memo it obtained that described Arabella's 2020 election agenda that included front groups that quickly closed once the election passed. The memo to megadonors purported to try to combat "political fearmongering," "attacks on voter registration," "viral misinformation," "disputes regarding election results," and "post-Election Day violence."[400]

It seems absurd for a powerful branch of the suppression hysteria industry to raise a red flag about "political fearmongering" and "viral misinformation."

Here are some of the Arabella groups that promote "fearmongering" for the purpose of securing elections for Democrats.

- Voting Rights Lab is a project of the New Venture Fund. The lobbying arm, Voting Rights Action, is fiscally sponsored by Arabella Advisor's Sixteen Thirty Fund. Funders for the Voting Rights Lab, through the New Venture Fund, include the Peter E. Haas Jr. Family Fund, which gave $50,000 to the New Venture Fund earmarked for the Voting Rights Lab, according to its financial disclosure report to the IRS in 2020.[401] Named for the Levi Strauss executive, the Haas organization says it seeks "equity in education and health, and to foster transformation in community norms."[402]

- Another funder for this group is the Sarah Min and Matt Pincus Foundation, a Delaware-based nonprofit that has donated to Planned Parenthood, the League of Conservation Voters, and other groups on the left, which gave $50,000 to the Voting Rights Lab in 2020.[403]

- The Wellspring Philanthropic Fund gave $310,000 to the Voting Rights Lab.[404] Created in 2001 as a secretive network of grantmaking organizations, Wellspring was funded by three hedge fund billionaires: Andrew Shechtel, David Gelbaum, and C. Frederick Taylor, according to the Capital Research Center.[405]

- Democracy Funders Collaborative Census Subgroup, better known simply as the Democracy Funders Collaborative, is a group of left-of-center grant makers that came together in 2015 to plan a strategy for the 2020 Census count and how to gear it toward helping Democrats. The Democracy Funders Collaborative should not be confused with the Democracy Alliance, which also describes itself as a collaborative. The Democracy Funders Collaborative is a project of the New Venture Fund. Its donors included some of the usuals, such as the Democracy Fund, a separate group founded by eBay co-founder and left-wing billionaire Pierre Omidyar, and the Wellspring Philanthropic Fund.

- The Democracy Fund and the Wellspring Philanthropic Fund teamed with the Spitzer Trust—the family foundation of the disgraced former New York governor—to establish the Trusted Elections Fund in 2020.[406] The Trusted Elections Fund, a project of the New Venture Fund, supposedly had the goal to address "election crises." or contested election results.[407] The fund was run by director Jennifer Flanagan, a former deputy secretary of state in Colorado.[408]

- In June 2020, the William and Flora Hewlett Foundation, a nonprofit established in 1966 by Hewlett-Packard co-founder William Hewlett, gave the New Venture Fund a $1 million grant earmarked to boost the Trusted Election Fund.[409] The Hewlett Foundation makes donations in a left-leaning direction on issues concerning education, the environment, and global development.

- Other significant donors to the Trusted Elections Fund included $150,000 from the Joyce Foundation, another reoccurring donor, "to support a safe, smooth, and trusted post-election period."[410] Despite so much money from so many august sources, the Trusted Elections Fund seemed to shut down after the 2020 election was over—not unusual for Arabella network-sponsored groups. Trump was defeated, so the group wasn't needed any longer.[411]

- Democracy for All 2021 Action is a project of the Sixteen Thirty Fund that lobbies for automatic and Election Day voter registration, while opposing ID laws. The organization is officially a coalition of twenty groups that include the Elizabeth Warren-aligned think tank Demos that designed a Biden administration executive action on voter registration, the identity politics group Color of Change, and other organizations. Deirdre Schifeling is the founder and campaign director of Democracy for All 2021 Action. Schifeling was also the leader of the Fight Back Table, which was a group preparing for "mass public unrest" in 2020 if Trump was re-elected.[412]

- The Fair Elections Center has also promoted suppression hysteria. Founded as a New Venture Fund fiscally-sponsored group in 2006, the organization spun off into an individual organization in 2018.

- The Fidelity Investments Charitable Gift Fund, one of the largest corporate donors to the Brennan Center, gave $1.2 million in 2018 and 2019 to the Fair Elections Center. The Everett B. and Patti Birch Foundation, a New York-based nonprofit established in 1992, donated $500,000 to the Fair Elections Center, according to the Capital Research Center. The Birch Foundation has reportedly donated more than $6 million to voter registration and education activities.[413]

- The Carnegie Corporation of New York, founded in 1911 by Andrew Carnegie, contributed more than $200,000 to the Fair Elections Center. In recent decades, the Carnegie Corporation has contributed heavily to Alliance for Justice, which pushes Democrat-appointed judges, the now-defunct Association for Community Organizers for Reform Now, and the Mexican American Legal Defense and Education Fund.[414]

- The Heinz Endowments, associated with the Heinz Ketchup company, made two separate contributions of $124,000 and $45,000 to the Fair Elections Center. Heinz Endowments has separately been a leading funder of Pennsylvania environmental groups.[415]

- The George Gund Foundation, a left-leaning Ohio-based organization that supports a "wealth tax," environmental programs, and criminal justice reform, contributed $200,000 to the Fair Elections Center.[416] The Kresge Foundation, a Michigan-based group that takes left-leaning positions on illegal immigration, race, and environmental matters, donated $100,000 to the Fair Elections Center.[417]

- The aforementioned Democracy Fund gave $75,000 to the Fair Elections Center.

- Arabella's Sixteen Thirty Fund also gave heavily pass-through donations for get-out-the-vote operations. It sent $174 million in 2020 to America Votes, which bills itself as the "coordination hub of the progressive community.[418] The organization was created ahead of the 2004 election geared at defeating George W. Bush.[419]

- America Votes was founded as a coalition of Democrat activists, including Partnership for America's Families President Steve Rosenthal, EMILY's List founder Ellen Malcolm, former Clinton administration official Harold Ickes, then-Service Employees International Union president Andy Stern, and Sierra Club Executive Director Carl Pope.[420] Politico described America Votes as a "liberal umbrella group that works on voter registration and turnout and collaborates with other political groups across the left."[421]

- The Center for Secure and Modern Elections is another project of the New Venture Fund and advocates for automatic voter registration, more mail-in voting, and even weaker penalties for lying on voter registration forms.[422] It also has a "sister" lobbying organization, CSME Action, which is part of the Sixteen Thirty Fund.

- It has close ties with non-Arabella linked Center for Tech and Civic Life, the organization that got $350 million from Facebook founder Mark Zuckerberg to fund election administration to drive up the Democrat vote in 2020.

- As a pass-through organization, the CSME doesn't have to set up status with the IRS or disclose donors, however, several organizations have publicly announced donations aimed at boosting the CSME. These include the Bauman Foundation, which gave $25,000 in 2016.[423] Also, the Democracy Fund, associated with Omidyar, gave $100,000 to the New Venture Fund for funding the CSME. The Democracy Fund Voice, the 501(c)(4) lobbying arm of the Democracy Fund, donated $1 million to CSME Action.[424]

- In 2020, the Joyce Foundation gave $600,000 to the New Venture Fund "to support expanding the Center for Secure and Modern Elections' Cities Project to give support to elections jurisdictions" in battlegrounds of Wisconsin, Michigan, Minnesota, and Ohio for the November 2020 election.[425] The Blaustein Foundation gave $200,000 toward the CSME in 2020 in "support of the Cities Project" for the purpose of voter engagement in large cities.[426]

- The Wellspring Philanthropic Fund also gave $1 million to the New Venture Fund to expand mail-in voting, some of which likely went to the CSME, but was perhaps spread across the other New Venture voting groups.[427]

- While short of the Mark Zuckerberg fortune dumped into running elections, the Arabella network also gave $25 million to the Center for Tech and Civic Life.[428] The Capital Research Center determined a link between the CTCL and the CSME. Sam Oliker-Friedland, CSME's chief counsel by 2020, had previously worked for the digital campaign training group New Organization Institute, which founded the CTCL.[429]

- The Freedom to Vote Alliance is an organization that seemed to pop up in 2022, claiming to be business and civic leaders committed to stopping state voter suppression laws. It seems to have had a healthy advertising budget in Washington, sponsoring ads with Politico and other outlets that reach influencers.

- In January 2022, the group organized a letter signed by forty heads of companies and nonprofit groups to President Joe Biden and Senate leaders calling for changing the Senate rules to pass the John Lewis Voting Rights Advancement Act and the Freedom to Vote Act. Signers included Stacy Schusterman, chairman of Samson Energy and the leader of the alliance; Eric Schmidt, former CEO of Google; Robert Smith, CEO of Vista Equity Partners; and Josh Silverman, CEO of Etsy.[430]

- While the Freedom to Vote Alliance doesn't appear to be singularly an Arabella-sponsored enterprise, it does have a link. The keyword is "alliance," as the website says its "partners" are the Black Economic Alliance, Leadership Now, and Small Business for America's Future.[431] Small Business for America's Future is a project of Arabella's Sixteen Thirty Fund and was originally established to oppose the Trump 2017 Tax Cuts and Jobs Act.[432]

- The Rockefeller Brothers Fund, a separate entity from the Rockefeller Family Fund, donated $25,000 in 2018 and $250,000 in 2019 to the New Venture Fund that was earmarked for "elections and voting rights."[433] The Rockefeller Brothers Fund, started in the 1940s by the sons of John D. Rockefeller, has become a far-left group and uses its money to advocate for environmental policy and anti-Israel, pro-Palestinian policies. In 2019, before the Zuckerberg contributions, the Rockefeller Brothers Fund gave $150,000 to the Center for Tech and Civic Life.

- The New Venture Fund also launched Voter Rights Action, with Democrat political veteran Laura Packard as the founder and seemingly the only person involved in the organization. In 2016, Packard delivered about five hundred thousand signatures on a petition to the Justice Department demanding an investigation of what she said were voter suppression cases in Arizona and Alabama, when she worked on behalf of MoveOn. Voter Rights Action lent its support and signature to voting legislation in states across the country. But like many Arabella network groups after an election cycle wraps up, Voter Rights Action appears to have folded up by early 2020, with no new content on Twitter or Facebook pages.[434]

There are numerous other organizations not aligned with the Arabella Advisors network that push the narrative of a rampant crisis to stop people from voting. Below are a few more examples regarding groups that focus heavily on election policy.

Voter Protection Project

The Voter Protection Project, a political action committee, is part of the Progressive State Leaders Committee.[435] Andrew Janz, a former deputy district attorney in Fresno County, California, founded the Voter Protection Project in 2019.[436]

The PAC spent $494,000 on trying to elect Democrats opposed to election security measures. After that, $5.2 million was spent on media buys.[437]

Some of the donors to the Voter Protection Project include $865,595 from Bold PAC, a super PAC that focuses on getting Hispanic Democrats elected to Congress; $50,000 from the House Majority PAC, which focuses on helping Democrats get elected and re-elected to Congress; and $30,000 from the Democrat-aligned Congressional Black Caucus PAC.[438]

Common Cause

Common Cause, a 501(c)(4) policy advocacy group, has historically focused on campaign finance, fighting corruption, and "good government" policies. But Common Cause also sponsors the Protect the Vote Project that included more than sixty-thousand "election protection volunteers" across the country in 2020 to monitor polling locations and had a hotline to report cases of perceived voter suppression.[439]

Though Common Cause projects itself as a white-hat nonpartisan group, George Soros's Open Society Foundations has given Common Cause more than $2 million since 2000. Since 2009, the Soros-sponsored Foundation to Promote an Open Society has given $600,000 to Common Cause.[440]

Common Cause is funded by other traditionally big left-wing donors such as the Arca Foundation, which has given $1.4 million to the watchdog group since 2000. Arca has also contributed to the Center for American Progress, Demos, Color of Change, and other groups on the left. The Carnegie Corporation of New York, another common donor to such causes, gave $1.8 million over the last two decades. The San Francisco-based James Irvine Foundation, which gives to pro-labor union groups such as the National Employment Law Project and the anti-fossil fuels Liberty Hill Foundation, has donated $1.37 million to Common Cause since 2005. The Ford Foundation, another common donor to left-leaning causes, has contributed $685,000 to Common Cause since 2000. The Robert Wood Johnson Foundation, which usually promotes left-leaning health care policies, has given $309,093 to Common Cause since 2002.[441]

Corporate donors included Fidelity Investments Charitable Gift Fund (again) giving $579,500 since 2003 and the Vanguard Charitable Endowment Program, the fourth largest manager of donor-advised funds in the nation, which has also donated to politically-charged groups such as Planned Parenthood and the League of Women Voters, has given $506,500 since 2006 to Common Cause.

Department of Labor documents show that the Communications Workers of America contributed $55,000 to Common Cause. The California Nurses Association, the United Food and Commercial Workers Local 555, and the SEIU Illinois State Council also reportedly contributed to Common Cause.[442]

iVote Fund

iVote Fund is a political action committee founded in 2014 that focuses on automatic voter registration. Ellen Kurz is the founder of the organization.[443]

iVote Fund routinely claims Republican secretaries of state engage in supposed "voter suppression," and it objects to voter ID laws and voter roll maintenance. The group funds Democrat candidates in secretary of state races across the country—as at least until recently, these contests have gotten very little attention. The PAC also pushes ballot initiatives and helps laws get passed in a dozen states and the District of Columbia.[444]

The largest individual donor to the PAC is Carolyn G. Mugar, with Farm Aid, who contributed $108,000 in the 2018 election cycle, according to FEC records. American Bridge 21st Century is the biggest iVote funder, giving separate donations of $250,000, $200,000, $300,000, $325,000 and $435,000 in 2018. Another donor, AFT Solidarity—a super PAC affiliated with the American

Federations of Teachers—gave $50,000 to iVote in 2018.[445] This is followed by other prominent left-wing organizations such as the National Education Association, EMILY's List, Let America Vote, Priorities USA Action, and Unite Here.[446]

All Voting is Local

The Leadership Conference Education Fund launched All Voting is Local in 2018 to focus on pushing mail-in voting and increasing the number of polling and ballot drop-off locations. The group contacts voters who were removed from voter registration rolls. It has also opposed voter ID. The group, run by former Clinton and Obama presidential campaign aide Hannah Fried, had claimed one million voters were unable to vote in the 2016 election.[447]

In addition to the Leadership Conference, All Voting is Local operates as a collaborative of several key left-of-center groups such as the American Civil Liberties Union, the American Constitution Society, the Campaign Legal Center, and the Lawyers' Committee for Civil Rights Under Law.[448]

Voting Rights Institute

The Voting Rights Institute was founded by the left-leaning American Constitution Society for Law and Policy and the Campaign Legal Center. It is operated at the Georgetown University Law Center. The institute was started in response to the Supreme Court's *Shelby County v. Holder* decision in 2013. The institute has been funded by traditional donors to progressive groups such as the aforementioned John D. and Catherine T. MacArthur Foundation, the Rockefeller Brothers Fund, and the Wallace Global Fund.[449]

Secure Democracy

Secure Democracy, established in 2018, professes to support expanding early voting and mail-in ballot drop boxes, and focuses on restoring the right of released prisoners to vote. The organization doesn't have to disclose donors. But it shared a physical address with the Not Who We Are PAC, which was funded by a group of Silicon Valley billionaires that included Pierre Omidyar, who gave $200,000 to the organization; Dustin Moskovitz, who was among the Facebook founders and contributed $125,000; Moskovitz's wife Cari Tuna, who contributed $125,000; and Christopher Hughes, also a Facebook co-founder, who contributed $250,000 to Secure Democracy.[450]

The Unite America PAC—which supports expanding mail-in voting, nonpartisan primaries, and ranked-choice voting among other issues—gave $700,000 to Secure Democracy. The North Star Fund—financed in part by the Ford Foundation and George Soros's Foundation to Promote Open Society—gave $1 million in 2020 to Secure Democracy.[451]

The Left has an agenda for controlling elections, has a chief spokesperson, and has billions of dollars backing its agenda to enact a nationalized political machine.

Democracy has thus far survived an onslaught from HR 1 and other legislation to warp elections. But unscrupulous politicians using lofty language will continue to try to ram through such legislation with feel-good titles that would have the end result of opening up elections to chaos and fraud.

Election bills can temporarily die. Fiery spokespersons such as Stacey Abrams can come and go. That leaves the deep-pocketed left-wing advocacy groups and their billionaire funders as the bulwark that will keep the insidious aspirations of a nationalized Tammany Hall going. It's ultimately up to the citizenry to demand clean and trustworthy elections.

Stopping Tammany Hall 2.0

I f democracy relies on the consent of the losers accepting defeat, the prospects didn't sound promising when President Joe Biden said months before the 2022 midterm elections: "I'm not going to say it's going to be legit. The increase and the prospect of being illegitimate is in direct proportion to us not being able to get these reforms passed."

Biden was talking about the collapse of Democrat election overhaul legislation.

Legislation to essentially codify Tammany Hall 2.0 nationally was thwarted, but only by a Senate filibuster. Perhaps a new majority in Congress will delay such an obscene power grab as HR 1 from passing—but majorities see-saw back and forth, and Democrats certainly smell blood.

It is remarkable how the arguments and goals of the machines have remained the same over the years, even if the language, framing, and selling points have slightly altered. The political machines of the past pushed for immigration mills for signing up voters, immediately enfranchising the incarcerated or formerly incarcerated, and of course, smearing every reform from the secret ballot and requiring voter registration to voter ID.

While Mark Zuckerberg announced that he won't fund future elections, one nationalized machine-style development in 2022 that should be of concern has been an effort to take over local election offices on a two front effort. The Run for Something PAC established the "Clerk Work" program as a three-year eighty-million-dollar project to get liberal activists elected as election clerks. In that same vein, the Center for Tech and Civic Life—which administered the Zuckerberg grants in 2020—teamed with other left-leaning election groups to launch the US Alliance for Election Excellence, a five-year eighty-million-dollar project geared at training and advising local election offices on how to run elections. It's a safe bet that advice will not be entirely objective.

The answer shouldn't be for a new Republican majority in Congress to impose their own alternative version of HR 1. Politicians being politicians will craft a bill that is advantageous to their party and not so much to the electorate. Just as Democrats don't necessarily care about voting rights, Republicans don't necessarily care about election integrity. Both sides care most about winning and want a leg up. But Republicans know they are on defense, as history tells us Democrats are better at stealing elections.

While a national voter ID requirement might seem desirable, elections are best handled by the states. The federal government's primary responsibility is to enforce the Fourteenth and Fifteenth Amendments as voting rights go. The Left has unfortunately bastardized—and weaponized—the phrase "voting rights" to achieve a partisan agenda of what they believe will produce a permanent Democrat majority.

The 2021 state laws were a good start in building faith in elections.

After mail-in voting surpassed in-person voting in the 2020 election, it prompted state action. Sure, providing an ID number when voting by mail or showing one before in-person voting makes it more difficult to vote than just showing up and voting. Requiring voters to be registered before voting also makes voting more difficult than just casting a ballot. The same could be said of requiring someone to live in the jurisdiction where they vote.

It poses more of a burden for voters to go to the election worker's table and have their name crossed off a list than if they could just walk straight into the voting booth. All these rules could be accurately called "restrictive." That doesn't make any of them vote denial, voter intimidation, or voter dilution, which violate federal law. "Suppression" again, is a focus-grouped catch-all term to blur the lines between what's legal and illegal.

Somewhere along the way, a civilized functional republic must establish a process—even if that process creates a modicum of inconvenience—to uphold the public's confidence.

A simple change would be to ensure election laws on the books are enforced.

What happened in Pennsylvania during 2020 was particularly alarming; for a governor to essentially set aside election laws—with an assist from the elected Supreme Court—against the will of the legislature is a big problem. Lawmakers in Pennsylvania and other state legislatures should claw back authority over elections from the executive branch to ensure that such unilateral power grabs don't happen again.

Many states blocked private money from funding election administration. But not enough states. There could also be a place for federal action.

Rep. Claudia Tenney, R-NY, co-chair of the House Election Integrity Caucus, proposed amending the Internal Revenue Code to prohibit tax exempt organizations from providing direct funding to official election organizations or to pay for election administration. This would be perfectly appropriate and within bounds of federal law.[452] This would allow Congress to address tax exemption law without micromanaging the administration of elections, which should usually be the purview of the states.

This isn't the only area in which to consider federal action.

The gravest challenge to honest elections is vote trafficking. The most recent trafficking scandal was in 2018, and the election was voided because North Carolina had an anti-ballot harvesting law. So many states do not. California, not surprisingly, even encourages harvesting. HR 1 would codify it nationally.

No politician could get away with passing a law allowing a political operative to follow a voter into a voting booth and stare over their shoulder as they cast a ballot. Yet, Democrats brazenly promote this as a positive good for mail-in voting. As was the case with the political machines in the 1800s, the secret ballot is an inconvenience for some politicians.

Mostly red states have restricted harvesting based on the number of ballots someone can return and from who, such as family members. So, this would not suppress voting but would prevent voter intimidation or outright ballot theft. Although mostly red states have taken the initiative, Democrat voters and others in blue states should have their rights protected as well.

While I'm leery of federal legislation, a carefully-tailored national ban on vote trafficking could be consistent with the government's limited role of protecting the Fourteenth and Fifteenth Amendments. That's because harvesting encourages voter intimidation—thus could easily violate the right of someone voting for the candidate of their choice if facing the pressure of a hired political gun that shows up at their home.

There is legislation that stops short of a ban.

Rep. Rodney Davis, R-IL, introduced legislation in 2020 to discourage states from promoting ballot harvesting while still leaving it to the states to decide. The Davis bill would amend the Help America Vote Act to prohibit federal funds from the Election Assistance Commission from going to states that allow broad ballot harvesting. The Davis bill would allow for reasonable exception for employees of the US Postal Service, family members of the voter, household members of the voter, and caregivers of the voter.[453]

If Republicans retake the majority of both houses of Congress, they should pass the Tenney legislation on Zuckerbucks and the Davis bill on ballot harvesting. They should then challenge President Joe Biden to defend his veto of legislation that would likely have broad public support.

Ballot trafficking wouldn't be as much of a problem without such a dramatic expansion of mail-in voting, set to surpass in-person voting. In 2020, Democrats did not let the COVID-19 pandemic go to waste.

Three-fourths of the public support voter ID laws, and this is usually thought of in the context of in-person voting. This makes sense for all mail-in ballots as well and has been at the core of most of the major state reforms.

Somewhere on this side of "release the kraken" and the horrific January 6 Capitol riot, many election integrity advocates have understandably become shy about pushing forward. Kooky conspiracies that get floated should be rejected. But the Right is frequently deterred from the mission to avoid being lumped in with crazies.

The Left has never seemed to mind jumping in the same pool with crazies and plows forward with an agenda, usually with a wink to the conspiracy nuts. Even before Democrats raised Stacey Abrams up as a hero, a fringe of Democrats had long insisted dark conspiracies were behind Republican victories.

After the tumultuous 2000 election, House Democrats made twenty objections to the certification of George W. Bush's electoral votes in January 2001. No Senate Democrat sponsored the objection, so they were unable to debate on the matter. The 2000 election was so unusual, Democrats can get a pass. But in 2004, many Democrats rallied behind wild stories about crooked voting machines in Ohio that rigged the election for Bush's victory over John Kerry. During a joint session of Congress in January 2005, Ohio Rep. Stephanie Tubbs Jones made an objection to certifying Ohio's electoral votes. California Democrat Sen. Barbara Boxer sponsored the objection, which forced two hours of debate in each chamber of Congress. Flipping Ohio would have changed the result of the 2004 election, but the effort failed.

During the joint session to certify the electoral votes in January 2017, House Democrats made eleven objections to certifying the victory of Donald Trump in battleground states but also in such states as Mississippi, Alabama, and Wyoming—states where Trump beat Clinton by about twenty points or more. Unlike in 2005, there was no Senate sponsor.

For the joint session on January 6, 2021, Republicans were, for the first time, going to do what Democrats have done with every Republican victory since 2000. In this case, though, more than one hundred GOP House members signed on to objections to certification of some of the close states. A handful of senators announced they would be sponsoring the challenges to force two hours of debate. There was never a chance of flipping the election. Though—had it not been for the riot—the assorted election oddities of 2020 would have been debated during the daylight and perhaps into prime time since four disputed states were expected to get two hours of debate each. Trump's grievances would have been aired. Instead, what debate occurred was well after midnight.

There is some bipartisan support in Congress to scrap the Electoral Count Act. The law was enacted after the disputed 1876 election to give Congress the authority to count, challenge, and certify Electoral College votes and settle disputes. The intent of the law was in the unlikely event that states send competing sets of electors to Washington. Such a bill could have passed with a bipartisan majority, but Senate Majority Leader Chuck Schumer blocked it because he wanted a more sweeping election overhaul.

Even if the awful events of January 6 never happened, it would be a good idea to scrap the Electoral Count Act. The law itself grants too much power to Congress. The beauty of the Electoral College is that it empowers states to choose the president. Moreover, Congress and the citizens should resist efforts to replace the Electoral College with a national popular vote for many reasons, but election security and voting rights are two. Under a popular vote system, fraudsters—or those seeking to engage in suppression—could rig an election by focusing on states and regions with the weakest security protocols. This type of plot could not succeed with the Electoral College in place. It's easy to predict the cities with the weakest election security to exploit. It's actually difficult to predict battleground states. At one point, Florida and Ohio were the ultimate prizes. Now the states are in the bag for Republicans. Before 2008, the state of Virginia was solidly red. Today it's as solidly blue in a presidential race as Massachusetts.

Obviously following the law is important. But so is sticking with facts above all else. Unfortunately, some quarters fuel conspiracy theories. This only undermines the case for stronger election integrity. The truth is on the side of advocates for election integrity and so is public opinion. There is no point in endangering that.

While the Left has the megaphones, the public generally gets it on issues.

The state of New York has taken some hits in these pages, not just for examples of recent corruption, but for the references to the legacy of Tammany Hall. But voters there showed good sense in November 2021, defeating three Democrat-backed constitutional amendments pitched as "voting rights" measures. The measures would have expanded absentee voting, allowed same-day voter registration, and changed the rules on drawing legislative districts—some of the same proposals Democrats in Congress sought to impose nationally. The state Republican party campaigned against the amendments, so there was no mistaking the partisan bent.

"New York, which is a 2 to 1 Democratic state, had three ballot measures and the people said they didn't want ballot harvesting, they wanted bipartisan redistricting and they did not want same day voter registration," Tenney said, a New York Republican and co-chair of the US House Election Integrity Caucus. "I think New York shows a good example that the people—regardless of party— want integrity in the voter rolls. But the Democrats have a loud voice in media, particularly. They dominate the corporate media. So they're able to demagogue this issue."

Outside the legislative realm, organizations such as the Public Interest Legal Foundation, the Honest Elections Project, and others should keep shining the light on problems and shame states and localities into doing the right thing on keeping clean voter lists.

History shows there have always been demagogues resisting changes to bring more integrity to elections. It's important the public arm itself with the facts—both historical and contemporary. This is the only way to combat the lies of the new political machine.

Endnotes

1   Douglass, Frederick, and John Lobb. The Life and Times of Frederick Douglass: From 1817-1882. Christian Age Office, 1882.

2   DePaolo, Joe. "Eric Swalwell Tells MSNBC That 2022 Could Be the 'Last' U.S. Election Ever if Democrats Don't Win." Mediaite. January 4, 2022. https://www.mediaite.com/news/eric-swalwell-tells-msnbc-that-2022-could-be-the-last-u-s-election-ever-if-democrats-dont-win/

3   "Voter Fraud." The Heritage Foundation. https://www.heritage.org/election-integrity/heritage-explains/voter-fraud

4   "Building Confidence in U.S. Elections." Report of Commission on Federal Election Reform. September 2005. https://www.eac.gov/sites/default/files/eac_assets/1/6/Exhibit%20M.PDF

5   Shapiro, Ilya. "The Voter Suppression Lie." *The Washington Examiner*. April 22, 2021. https://www.cato.org/commentary/voter-suppression-lie

6   Yee, Vivian. "Routine Voter Purge Is Cited in Brooklyn Election Trouble." *The New York Times*. April 22, 2016. https://www.nytimes.com/2016/04/23/nyregion/routine-voter-purge-is-cited-in-brooklyn-election-trouble.html

7   Levine, Jon. "Joe Biden spent decades warning of voter fraud — now called a myth by Dems." *New York Post*. September 19, 2020. https://nypost.com/2020/09/19/biden-spent-years-warning-of-voter-fraud-now-call-a-myth/

8   Ibid.

9   Adams, Christian. "The Myth of 'Voter Suppression.'" InsideSources. March 17, 2020. https://insidesources.com/the-myth-of-voter-suppression/

10   Blakemore, Erin. "Voter fraud used to be rampant. Now it's an anomaly." *National Geographic*. November 11, 2020. https://www.nationalgeographic.com/history/article/voter-fraud-used-to-be-rampant-now-an-anomaly

11   Ibid.

12   Fund, John and von Spakovsky, Hans. *Our Broken Elections: How the Left Changed the Way You Vote*. Encounter Books. November 2, 2021. Page 214.

13   Blakemore. "Voter fraud used to be rampant. Now it's an anomaly."

14   Fund, John. *Stealing Elections: How Voter Fraud Threatens Our Democracy*. Encounter Books. September 5, 2004. Page 8

15   Debats, Donald A. "Secrecy in Voting in American History: No Secrets There." The Institute for Advanced Technology in Humanities. University of Virginia. http://sociallogic.iath.virginia.edu/node/30

16   Debats, Donald A. "How the Other Half (plus) Voted: The Party Ticket States." The Institute for Advanced Technology in the Humanities. University of Virginia. http://sociallogic.iath.virginia.edu/node/31

17   Evans, Will. "Nineteenth-Century Political Ballots." Boston Athenaeum Digital Collections. https://cdm.bostonathenaeum.org/digital/collection/p16057coll29

18   Arablouei, Ramtin and Abdelfatah, Rund. "The History Of How We Vote: From Drunken Parties To Private Booths." NPR. October 26, 2020. https://www.npr.org/2020/10/26/927743294/the-history-of-how-we-vote-from-drunken-parties-to-private-booths

19   Debats. "How the Other Half (plus) Voted: The Party Ticket States."

20 Arablouei and Abdelfatah. "The History Of How We Vote: From Drunken Parties To Private Booths."

21 Ibid.

22 Fromer, Yoav. "Want to improve democracy? Abolish the secret ballot." *The Washington Post.* January 6, 2017. https://www.washingtonpost.com/posteverything/wp/2017/01/06/want-to-improve-democracy-abolish-the-secret-ballot/

23 Jacobson, Louis. "Steele says GOP fought hard for civil rights bills in 1960s." PolitiFact. May 25, 2010. https://www.politifact.com/factchecks/2010/may/25/michael-steele/steele-says-gop-fought-hard-civil-rights-bills-196/

24 "The For the People Act." Brennan Center for Justice. January 4, 2019. https://www.brennancenter.org/our-work/policy-solutions/for-the-people-act

25 Press Release. "Blunt Remarks Ahead of Democrats' Failed Push to Break Senate Rules, Force Through Election Takeover." January 19, 2022. https://www.blunt.senate.gov/news/videos/blunt-remarks-ahead-of-democrats-failed-push-to-break-senate-rules-force-through-election-takeover

26 "Jim Crow Laws." National Park Service. https://www.nps.gov/malu/learn/education/jim_crow_laws.htm

27 Blakemore. "Voter fraud used to be rampant. Now it's an anomaly."

28 von Spakovsky, Hans A. "Voter suppression? Dems flat-out wrong. Census data gives real story about US elections." Fox News. May 7, 2021. https://www.foxnews.com/opinion/voter-suppression-dems-wrong-census-elections-hans-von-spakovsky

29 Ibid.

30 Misra, Jordan. "Voter Turnout Rates Among All Voting Age and Major Racial and Ethnic Groups Were Higher Than in 2014." U.S. Census Bureau. April 23, 2019. https://www.census.gov/library/stories/2019/04/behind-2018-united-states-midterm-election-turnout.html

31   Segers, Grace. "Record voter turnout in 2018 midterm elections." CBS News. November 7, 2018. https://www.cbsnews.com/news/record-voter-turnout-in-2018-midterm-elections/

32   Krogstad, Jens Manuel; Noe-Bustamante, Luis; and Flores, Antonio. "Historic highs in 2018 voter turnout extended across racial and ethnic groups." Pew Research Center. May 1, 2019. https://www.pewresearch.org/fact-tank/2019/05/01/historic-highs-in-2018-voter-turnout-extended-across-racial-and-ethnic-groups/

33   Frey, William H. "2018 Voter Turnout Rose Dramatically for Groups Favoring Democrats, Census Confirms." Brookings Institution. May 2, 2019. https://www.brookings.edu/research/2018-voter-turnout-rose-dramatically-for-groups-favoring-democrats-census-confirms/

34   Curry, Tom. "Holder urges Congress to pass new voting protections." NBC News. July 16, 2013. https://www.nbcnews.com/politics/politics-news/holder-urges-congress-pass-new-voting-protections-flna6c10656131

35   "Voter Turnout." United States Elections Project. http://www.electproject.org/home/voter-turnout/voter-turnout-data

36   Ibid.

37   von Spakovsky, Hans. "Restoring the Voting Rights Act: Combating Discriminatory Abuses." Testimony before the Senate Committee on the Judiciary - Subcommittee on the Constitution. September 22, 2021. https://www.judiciary.senate.gov/imo/media/doc/Spakovsky%20Testimony.pdf

38   Farrell, Chris. "Mail-in Voting Fraud is Growing But Not New." *Daily Caller.* August 31, 2020. https://dailycaller.com/2020/08/31/farrell-mail-in-voting-fraud-is-growing-but-not-new/

39   Fund and von Spakovsky. Our Broken Elections.

40   Ryskind, Allan H. "Harpo Marx on election fraud." *The Washington Times.* November 1, 2016. https://www.washingtontimes.com/news/2016/nov/1/harpo-marx-on-election-fraud/

41 Nelson, Suzanne. "Congress Blasé About Carter-Baker." *Roll Call.* September 19, 2005. https://www.rollcall.com/2005/09/19/congress-blase-about-carter-baker/

42 Pan, Phillip P. "Naturalization: An Unnatural Process." *The Washington Post.* July 4, 2000. https://www.washingtonpost.com/archive/politics/2000/07/04/naturalization-an-unnatural-process/f5406f86-ba1f-431a-be13-09deae54c1ca/

43 Blakemore. "Voter fraud used to be rampant. Now it's an anomaly."

44 Fund, John. "How to Steal an Election." *City Journal.* Autumn 2004. https://www.city-journal.org/html/how-steal-election-12824.html

45 Hewitt, Hugh. *If It's Not Close, They Can't Cheat: Crushing the Democrats in Every Election and Why Your Life Depends on It.* Thomas Nelson Books. July 22, 2004.

46 Ibid.

47 Fund. *Stealing Elections.* Page 8.

48 Ibid.

49 Hewitt. *If It's Not Close, They Can't Cheat.*

50 Ibid.

51 Ibid.

52 Blakemore. "Voter fraud used to be rampant. Now it's an anomaly."

53 Crawford v. Marion County Election Board. 128 S. Ct. 1610, 1619 (2008). https://www.supremecourt.gov/opinions/07pdf/07-21.pdf

54 Interim Report of the Miami-Dade County Grand Jury, Inquiry into Absentee Ballot Voting, State Attorney Katherine Fernandez Rundle, Circuit Court of the Eleventh Judicial Circuit of Florida in and for the County of Miami-Dade, Fall Term A.D. 1997. February 2, 1998. http://miamisao.com/wp-content/uploads/2021/02/gj1997f-interim-1.pdf

55 Blakemore. "Voter fraud used to be rampant. Now it's an anomaly."

56   "William J. Brennan Center for Justice." Influence Watch. https://www.influencewatch.org/non-profit/william-j-brennan-center-for-justice/

57   Kroll, Alexander J. "Dismantling Self-Government: The Brennan Center's Election Fraud Offensive." Capital Research Center. April 1, 2014. https://capitalresearch.org/article/dismantling-self-government-the-brennan-centers-election-fraud-offensive/

58   "A Sampling of Recent Election Fraud Cases Across the United States." The Heritage Foundation. https://www.heritage.org/voterfraud

59   "Election Fraud Cases." The Heritage Foundation. https://www.heritage.org/voterfraud/search?combine=&state=All&year=&case_type=All&fraud_type=24497&page=0&_gl=1*90pcjb*_ga*YW1wLWFiRkVTS3ZuQUtsSmNEZTJKendTZ2c.*_ga_W14BT6YQ87*MTY0NzMxMjQ5Ni4xLjAuMTY0NzMxM-jQ5Ni42MA..&_ga=2.182046055.1169994175.1647312497-amp-abFESKvnAKlJcDe2JzwSgg

60   Ibid.

61   Queally, James. "Compton City Council election overturned in wake of vote rigging scandal." *The Los Angeles Times*. May 30, 2022. https://www.latimes.com/california/story/2022-05-30/compton-city-council-election-overturned

62   Satterfield, Jamie. "Ex-deputy blames 'infamous dirty politics' for vote-buying scheme in Monroe sheriff's race." *Knoxville News-Sentinel*. April 18, 2019. https://www.knoxnews.com/story/news/crime/2019/04/16/monroe-county-vote-buying-scheme-brian-wormy-hodge/3474977002/

63   "Voter Fraud Report: City of Mission, TX." The Heritage Foundation. https://www.heritage.org/voterfraud/9815

64   "Voter Fraud Report: North St. Louis." The Heritage Foundation. https://www.heritage.org/voterfraud/9029

65   "Voter Fraud Report: Thomas Ramey, Donald Whitten, and Jerry Bowman." The Heritage Foundation. https://www.heritage.org/voterfraud/9529

66   Fund. *Stealing Elections*.

67   Levitt, Justin. "The Truth About Voter Fraud." The Brennan Center for Justice. November 9, 2007. https://www.brennancenter.org/our-work/research-reports/truth-about-voter-fraud

68   Press Release. "Former U.S. Congressman and Philadelphia Political Operative Pleads Guilty to Election Fraud Charges." Department of Justice. June 6, 2022. https://www.justice.gov/usao-edpa/pr/former-us-congressman-and-philadelphia-political-operative-pleads-guilty-election-fraud

69   Lucas, Fred. "Biden Justice Department Advances Voter Fraud Case in Philadelphia Begun Under Trump." The Daily Signal. November 1, 2021. https://www.dailysignal.com/2021/11/01/biden-justice-department-advances-voter-fraud-case-in-philadelphia-begun-under-trump/ and; Fiorillo, Victor. "Mark Squilla Staffer Charged in South Philly Voter Fraud Conspiracy." *Philadelphia Magazine*. October 13, 2021. https://www.phillymag.com/news/2021/10/13/marie-beren-voter-fraud-mark-squilla/

70   AlSchmidt(@Commish_Schmidt).Twitter.October 27, 2021.https://twitter.com/Commish_Schmidt/status/1453442032974897152

71   Press Release. "AG Paxton Announces Joint Prosecution of Gregg County Organized Election Fraud in Mail-In Balloting Scheme." Texas Attorney General Ken Paxton. September 24, 2020. https://www.texasattorneygeneral.gov/news/releases/ag-paxton-announces-joint-prosecution-gregg-county-organized-election-fraud-mail-balloting-scheme

72   "Voter Fraud." The Heritage Foundation.

73   "Brooklyn Grand Jury Finds Fraud in 8 Primaries." *The New York Times*. September 5, 1984. https://www.nytimes.com/1984/09/05/nyregion/brooklyn-grand-jury-finds-fraud-in-8-primaries.html

74   "Voter Fraud." The Heritage Foundation.

75   Hupfer, Kyle. "Bad-Faith Democrat Attacks on Election Integrity Are Failing." RealClearPolitics. June 15, 2021. https://www.realclearpolitics.com/articles/2021/06/15/bad-faith_democrat_attacks_on_election_integrity_are_failing_145933.html

76   Transcript of "Remarks by President Biden on Protecting the Right to Vote." White House. January 11, 2022. Atlanta University Center Consortium. Atlanta, Georgia. https://www.whitehouse.gov/briefing-room/speeches-remarks/2022/01/11/remarks-by-president-biden-on-protecting-the-right-to-vote/

77   Gellman, Barton. "Trump's Next Coup Has Already Begun." *The Atlantic*. December 6, 2021. https://www.theatlantic.com/magazine/archive/2022/01/january-6-insurrection-trump-coup-2024-election/620843/

78   Berman, Ari. "The Coming Coup: How Republicans Are Laying the Groundwork to Steal Future Elections." Mother Jones. January 13, 2022. https://www.motherjones.com/politics/2022/01/how-republicans-are-taking-over-election-system-big-lie/

79   Riccardi, Nicholas. "'Slow-motion insurrection': Democracy experts alarmed over GOP takeover of election machinery." Associated Press via PBS. December 29, 2021. https://www.pbs.org/newshour/politics/slow-motion-insurrection-democracy-experts-alarmed-over-gop-takeover-of-election-machinery

80   Fowler, Stephen. "What Does Georgia's New Voting Law SB 202 Do?" Georgia Public Broadcasting. March 27, 2021. https://www.gpb.org/news/2021/03/27/what-does-georgias-new-voting-law-sb-202-do

81   Ibid.

82   Brumback, Kate. "Observer: Georgia county's elections messy, not fraudulent." Associated Press. June 16, 2021. https://apnews.com/article/donald-trump-ga-state-wire-georgia-elections-government-and-politics-87bb23d4d9b2ec80a1db715e6bf1c633

83   Press Release. "AMAC Joins Coalition to Support Safeguarding Arizona's Voter Registration Process." March 21, 2022. https://amac.us/amac-joins-coalition-to-support-safeguarding-arizonas-voter-registration-process/

84   "The Electoral College." National Conference of State Legislatures. November 11, 2020. https://www.ncsl.org/research/elections-and-campaigns/the-electoral-college.aspx

85   Fund. *Stealing Elections*.

86   McDaniel, Ronna. "Democrats Don't Want to Play by the Same Voting Rules." *The Washington Post*. August 27, 2020. https://www.washingtonpost.com/opinions/2020/08/27/ronna-mcdaniel-rnc-chairwoman-poll-watchers-voting/

87   Ehlke, Gretchen. "Men Get Jail Time In Milwaukee Tire-Slashing Case." Associated Press. April 26, 2006. http://web.archive.org/web/20060503003521/http://wfrv.com/topstories/local_story_116123954.html

88   "Former Justice Department Lawyer Accuses Holder of Dropping New Black Panther Case for Racial Reasons." Fox News. December 23, 2015. https://www.foxnews.com/politics/former-justice-department-lawyer-accuses-holder-of-dropping-new-black-panther-case-for-racial-reasons

89   Wagner, John. "Ex-Ehrlich Campaign Manager Schurick Convicted in Robocall Case." *The Washington Post*. December 6, 2011. https://www.washingtonpost.com/local/dc-politics/ex-ehrlich-campaign-manager-schurick-convicted-in-robocall-case/2011/12/06/gIQA6rNsaO_story.html

90   Press Release. "Record Early Voting Turnout Continues." Georgia Secretary of State. May 16, 2022. https://sos.ga.gov/news/record-early-voting-turnout-continues-2

91   "Myth vs. Fact: Misinformation About Florida's Election Reforms." Save Our Elections. Heritage Action. April 26, 2021. https://saveourelections.com/newsroom/myth-vs-fact-misinformation-on-floridas-election-reforms

92   Chen, Shawna. "Flood of CEOs, corporations speak out against Georgia's voting restrictions." Axios. April 2, 2021. https://www.axios.com/georgia-voting-restrictions-microsoft-corporations-57f321c3-f449-41c0-858e-02006d017768.html

93   Fowler. "What Does Georgia's New Voting Law SB 202 Do?"

94   Howell, Mike. "4 Myths About the Election Integrity Law in Georgia." Daily Signal. April 16, 2021. https://www.dailysignal.com/2021/04/16/heritage-foundation-fact-checks-the-rhetoric-on-georgia-election-reform-law/

95   von Spakovsky, Hans A. "The Big Lie About Texas and Other States' Election Reforms." The Heritage Foundation. July 19, 2021. https://www.heritage.org/election-integrity/commentary/the-big-lie-about-texas-and-other-states-election-reforms

96   Fowler. "What Does Georgia's New Voting Law SB 202 Do?"

97   Thrush, Glenn. "The N.A.A.C.P. and other civil rights groups sue Georgia to overturn a new law that limits voting." *The New York Times*. March 30, 2021. https://www.nytimes.com/2021/03/30/us/naacp-georgia-voting-rights-case.html

98   Fowler. "What Does Georgia's New Voting Law SB 202 Do?"

99   Ibid.

100 Payne, Daniel. "Reality check: What's really in the Texas voting reform bill?" Just the News. July 13, 2021. https://justthenews.com/government/state-houses/whats-texas-voting-reform-bill-made-democrats-flee-washington

101 Ura, Alexa. "What's in the new voting restriction legislation introduced in the Texas House and Senate." The Texas Tribune. July 8, 2021. https://www.texastribune.org/2021/07/08/texas-voting-bill-special-session/

102 von Spakovsky, Hans. "The Big Lie About Texas and Other States' Election Reforms." Fox News. July 16, 2021. https://www.foxnews.com/opinion/big-lie-texas-states-election-reforms-hans-von-spakovsky

103 Ibid.

104 Ibid.

105 Press Release. "Voters without photo ID may qualify for an exemption or free ID." Texas Secretary of State. October 23, 2015. https://www.sos.state.tx.us/about/newsreleases/2015/102315.shtml

106 von Spakovsky. "The Big Lie About Texas and Other States' Election Reforms."

107 Rove, Karl. "Blue-State Voter 'Suppression.'" *The Wall Street Journal*. March 24, 2021. https://www.wsj.com/articles/blue-state-voter-suppression-11616624579

108 Shapiro. "The Voter Suppression Lie."

109 Kessler, Glenn. "Biden falsely claims the new Georgia law 'ends voting hours early.'" *The Washington Post*. March 30, 2021. https://www.washingtonpost.com/politics/2021/03/30/biden-falsely-claims-new-georgia-law-ends-voting-hours-early/

110 Shapiro. "The Voter Suppression Lie."

111 Kertscher, Tom. "Did first-time use of photo ID cause 200,000 drop in Wisconsin voter turnout in presidential race?" PolitiFact. May 24, 2017. https://www.politifact.com/factchecks/2017/may/24/tammy-baldwin/photo-id-law-caused-200000-drop-wisconsin-voter-tu/

112 von Spakovsky, Hans and Janacek, Benjamin. "No, Hillary, Voter-ID Laws Don't 'Suppress' Turnout." National Review. June 20, 2017. https://www.nationalreview.com/2017/06/hillary-clinton-wisconsin-voter-suppression-claim-dubious-excuse-flawed-campaign/

113 Ibid.

114 "Building Confidence in U.S. Elections." Report of the Commission on Federal Election Reform.

115 Lee, Suevon and Smith, Sarah. "Everything You've Ever Wanted to Know About Voter ID Laws." Pro Publica. March 9, 2016. https://www.propublica.org/article/everything-youve-ever-wanted-to-know-about-voter-id-laws

116 Crawford v. Marion County Election Board. Supreme Court of the United States.

117 "Voter ID Laws." National Conference of State Legislatures. https://www.ncsl.org/research/elections-and-campaigns/voter-id.aspx

118 Fund, John and von Spakovsky, Hans. "Voter ID and the Real Threat to Democracy." *The Wall Street Journal*. August 1, 2016. https://www.wsj.com/articles/voter-id-and-the-real-threat-to-democracy-1470091513

119 Domonoske, Camila. "As November Approaches, Courts Deal Series Of Blows To Voter ID Laws." National Public Radio. August 2, 2016. https://www.npr.org/sections/thetwo-way/2016/08/02/488392765/as-november-approaches-courts-deal-series-of-blows-to-voter-id-laws

120 Schow, Ashe. "24 things that require a photo ID." *The Washington Examiner*. August 14, 2013. http://www.washingtonexaminer.com/24-things-that-require-a-photo-id/article/2534254

121 "Privileges and Immunities Clause." Cornell Law. https://www.law.cornell.edu/wex/privileges_and_immunities_clause

122 "Paul v. Virginia." U.S. Supreme Court. Justia. https://supreme.justia.com/cases/federal/us/75/168/

123 "Goldberg v. Kelly." U.S. Supreme Court. Justia. https://supreme.justia.com/cases/federal/us/397/254/

124 "Benefits - Verification Requirements." Virginia Department of Social Services. https://www.dss.virginia.gov/benefit/verification.cgi

125 Staff. "What Is a New York State Benefit Identification Card?" Reference.com. April 4, 2020. https://www.reference.com/world-view/new-york-state-benefit-identification-card-1ee295c76ec8481e

126 "Restrictions on Use of Public Assistance Electronic Benefit Transfer (EBT) Cards." National Conference of State Legislatures. December 12, 2019. https://www.ncsl.org/research/human-services/ebt-electronic-benefit-transfer-card-restrictions-for-public-assistance.aspx

127 Fleming, Esther. "What is the purpose of IDNYC?." SidmartinBio. February 23, 2021. https://www.sidmartinbio.org/what-is-the-purpose-of-idnyc/

128 "District of Columbia v. Heller." U.S. Supreme Court. Cornell Law School. June 26, 2008. https://www.law.cornell.edu/supct/html/07-290.ZO.html

129 "District of Columbia Gun Laws." Laws. December 22, 2019. http://gun.laws.com/state-gun-laws/district-of-columbia-gun-laws

130 "General Requirements for Firearms Registration." Metropolitan Police Department. http://mpdc.dc.gov/page/firearm-registration-general-requirements-study-guide

131 Rueb, Emily. "How Tough Is It? Buying a Gun in Oregon vs. New York City." *The New York Times*. October 9, 2015. https://www.nytimes.com/interactive/2015/10/09/nyregion/gun-laws-oregon-new-york-city.html?_r=0

132   "Lobbying Disclosures." Office of the Clerk of the House. http://
      lobbyingdisclosure.house.gov/register.html

133   "Lobbyist Registration Requirements." National Conference of
      State Legislatures. September 13, 2021. http://www.ncsl.org/
      research/ethics/50-state-chart-lobbyist-registration-require-
      ments.aspx

134   "Know Your Rights: Demonstrations and Protests." American
      Civil Liberties Union. https://www.aclu.org/sites/default/files/
      field_pdf_file/kyr_protests.pdf

135   "Loving v. Virginia." United States Supreme Court. Cornell Law
      School. https://www.law.cornell.edu/supremecourt/text/388/1

136   "Marriage License." Office of the City Clerk for the City of New
      York. https://www.cityclerk.nyc.gov/content/marriage-license

137   "Citizens Without Proof." Brennan Center for Justice at NYU
      School of Law. November 2006. https://www.brennancenter.org/
      sites/default/files/2020-09/download_file_39242.pdf

138   Press Release. "Public Supports Both Early Voting and Requiring
      Photo ID to Vote." June 21, 2021. https://www.monmouth.edu/
      polling-institute/reports/monmouthpoll_us_062121/

139   Samuels, Brett. "Poll finds growing support for voter ID require-
      ments." *The Hill*. August 18, 2021. https://thehill.com/home-
      news/campaign/568385-poll-finds-growing-support-for-voter-
      id-requirements

140   Rasmussen, Scott. "Election Reform Is a Winning Issue for
      Republicans." *National Review*. November 29, 2021. https://
      www.nationalreview.com/2021/11/election-reform-is-a-win-
      ning-issue-for-republicans/

141   Cantoni, Enrico and Pons, Vincent. "Strict ID Laws Don't Stop
      Voters: Evidence from a U.S. Nationwide Panel, 2008–2018."
      National Bureau of Economic Research. February 2019. https://
      www.nber.org/papers/w25522

142   Lopez, German. "A new study finds voter ID laws don't reduce
      voter fraud — or voter turnout." Vox. February 21, 2019. https://
      www.vox.com/policy-and-politics/2019/2/21/18230009/voter-
      id-laws-fraud-turnout-study-research

143 Morrison, Caleb and von Spakovsky, Hans. "New Study Confirms Voter ID Laws Don't Hurt Election Turnout." The Daily Signal. February 26, 2019. https://www.dailysignal.com/2019/02/26/new-study-confirms-voter-id-laws-dont-hurt-election-turnout/

144 Misra. "Voter Turnout Rates Among All Voting Age and Major Racial and Ethnic Groups Were Higher Than in 2014."

145 "Voter ID Laws Don't Depress Turnout." Honest Elections Project. January 9, 2020. https://www.honestelections.org/voter-id-laws-dont-depress-turnout/

146 Hajnal, Zoltan; Lajevardi, Nazita and Nielson, Lindsay. "Voter Identification Laws and the Suppression of Minority Votes." *University of Chicago Press Journal.* https://www.journals.uchicago.edu/doi/abs/10.1086/688343

147 Grimmer, Justin; Hersh, Eitan; Meredith, Marc; Mummolo, Jonathan; Nall, Clayton. "Comment on 'Voter Identification Laws and the Suppression of Minority Votes.'" Stanford University. August 7, 2017. http://stanford.edu/~jgrimmer/comment_final.pdf

148 Frank, John. "Colorado reports nearly 29,000 rejected ballots in 2020 election, with younger voters the bulk of total." *The Colorado Sun.* December 9, 2020. https://coloradosun.com/2020/12/09/colorado-rejected-ballots-2020-election/

149 Contorno, Steve. "DeSantis wants voters' signatures to match. Would his pass the test?" *Tampa Bay Times.* April 13, 2021. https://www.tampabay.com/news/florida-politics/2021/04/13/desantis-wants-voters-signatures-to-match-would-his-pass-the-test/

150 Lott, John R. "America the Outlier: Voter Photo IDs Are the Rule in Europe and Elsewhere." RealClearInvestigations. June 1, 2021. https://www.realclearinvestigations.com/articles/2021/06/01/the_us_is_a_voter_photo_id_outlier_theyre_the_rule_in_europe_and_elsewhere_778714.html

151 "Carter promotes requirement of voter ID." *Dalton Daily Citizen.* March 23, 2006. https://www.dailycitizen.news/news/carter-promotes-requirement-of-voter-id/article_8c87793c-f62c-56b0-9210-0b6e1a5fdf2a.html

152 von Spakovsky, Hans. "Ensuring the Integrity of Our Election System." The Heritage Foundation. October 6, 2020. https://www.heritage.org/election-integrity/commentary/ensuring-the-integrity-our-election-system

153 Silva, Christianna and Simon, Scott. "In New Documentary, Stacey Abrams Probes The State Of Voter Suppression In 2020." NPR. September 5, 2020. https://www.npr.org/2020/09/05/909969046/stacey-abrams-discusses-voter-suppression-and-her-new-documentary-appearance

154 "Vote Purges." The Brennan Center for Justice. https://www.brennancenter.org/issues/ensure-every-american-can-vote/vote-suppression/voter-purges

155 Masterson, Matthew. "Voter fraud can be prevented with right tools." *The Washington Times*. March 13, 2017. https://www.washingtontimes.com/news/2017/mar/13/voter-fraud-can-be-prevented-with-right-tools/

156 "Surveys and Data." U.S. Election Assistance Administration. https://www.eac.gov/research-and-data/datasets-codebooks-and-surveys

157 Press Release. "Lawsuit to Remove Dead Voters in Pennsylvania Ends With Win for Election Integrity." Public Interest Legal Foundation. April 7, 2021. https://publicinterestlegal.org/press/lawsuit-to-remove-dead-voters-in-pennsylvania-ends-with-win-for-election-integrity/

158 Press Release. "Detroit Voter Cleanup Lawsuit Ends." Public Interest Legal Foundation. June 30, 2020. https://publicinterestlegal.org/press/detroit-voter-roll-cleanup-lawsuit-ends/

159 Fund, John and von Spakovsky, Hans. "Voter fraud exists—Even though many in the media claim it doesn't." Fox News. October 27, 2018. https://www.foxnews.com/opinion/voter-fraud-exists-even-though-many-in-the-media-claim-it-doesnt

160 Lucas, Fred. "Mayoral Candidate in Texas Charged With Over 100 Counts of Voter Fraud." The Daily Signal. October 9, 2020. https://www.dailysignal.com/2020/10/09/mayoral-candidate-in-texas-charged-with-over-100-counts-of-voter-fraud/

161 Bahl, Andrew. "Former Congressman Steve Watkins agrees to diversion deal, could avoid prosecution." *Topeka Capital-Journal*. March 2, 2021. https://www.cjonline.com/story/news/politics/elections/2021/03/02/former-congressman-steve-watkins-agrees-deal-avoiding-prosecution/6894378002/

162 "DOI To Board Of Elections: Get Dead People Off Voter Rolls." CBS News. December 30, 2013. https://www.cbsnews.com/newyork/news/doi-to-board-of-elections-get-dead-people-off-voter-rolls/

163 Fritze, John. "Wendy Rosen reaches plea agreement on voting charges." *The Baltimore Sun*. March 8, 2013. https://www.baltimoresun.com/politics/bal-wendy-rosen-reaches-plea-agreement-on-voting-charges-20130308-story.html

164 Ervin, Keith. "Seven charged in vote-fraud scheme." *The Seattle Times*. July 27, 2007. https://www.seattletimes.com/seattle-news/seven-charged-in-vote-fraud-scheme/

165 "Building Confidence in U.S. Elections." Report of the Commission on Federal Election Reform.

166 von Spakovsky. "Ensuring the Integrity of Our Election System."

167 Fund and von Spakovsky. "Voter fraud exists—Even though many in the media claim it doesn't."

168 Issue Brief. "Inaccurate, Costly, and Inefficient." Pew Center for the States. February 2012. www.pewtrusts.org/~/media/legacy/uploadedfiles/pcs_assets/2012/pewupgradingvoterregistrationpdf.pdf

169 von Spakovsky, Hans. "H.R. 1 Is a Threat to American Democracy. Period." *The National Interest*. March 10, 2021. https://nationalinterest.org/feature/hr-1-threat-american-democracy-period-179804

170 Press Release. "Judicial Watch Study: 1.8 Million Extra Registered Voters." Judicial Watch. October 16, 2020. https://www.judicialwatch.org/judicial-watch-study/

171 Press Release. "Judicial Watch: Pennsylvania Counties Admit They Gave Incorrect Voter Roll Information to Federal Government—Disclose Conflicting Numbers of Inactive Voters to Court." Judicial Watch. October 2, 2020. https://www.judicial-watch.org/penn-counties-incorrect-voter-info/

172 "Under Threat Of Lawsuit, Allegheny Co. Purging 69,000 Inactive Voters From Rolls." CBS 2 Pittsburgh. January 14, 2020. https://pittsburgh.cbslocal.com/2020/01/14/allegheny-county-board-of-elections-voter-rolls/

173 Press Release. "Judicial Watch Study: 1.8 Million Extra Registered Voters."

174 Press Release. "244 Counties Have More Registered Voters Than Live Adults." Public Interest Legal Foundation. August 19, 2019. https://publicinterestlegal.org/press/244-counties-have-more-registered-voters-than-live-adults/

175 Ibid.

176 Ibid.

177 "North Carolina Election Officials Have Been Put on Notice: Clean Up Voter Rolls or Face Lawsuits." Honest Elections Project. May 5, 2020. https://www.honestelections.org/north-carolina-election-officials-have-been-put-on-notice-clean-up-voter-rolls-or-face-lawsuits/

178 Morrison, Micah. "Ballot Update: Judicial Watch Cleans Up Dirty Voter Rolls." Judicial Watch. October 15, 2020. https://www.judicialwatch.org/ballot-update-judicial-watch-cleans-up-dirty-voter-rolls/

179 Press Release. "Judicial Watch Warns 14 Counties in Five States to Clean Voter Registration Lists or Face Federal Lawsuits." Judicial Watch. November 16, 2021. https://www.judicialwatch.org/jw-14-counties-5-states/

180 Crabtree, Susan. "Calif. Begins Removing 5 Million Inactive Voters on Its Rolls." RealClearPolitics. June 20, 2019. https://www.realclearpolitics.com/articles/2019/06/20/calif_begins_removing_5_million_inactive_voters_on_its_rolls__140602.html

181 Press Release. "Judicial Watch Warns 14 Counties in Five States to Clean Voter Registration Lists or Face Federal Lawsuits."

182 Ibid.

183 Masterson. "Voter fraud can be prevented with right tools."

184 Ibid.

185 Biesecker, Michael; Drew, Jonathan and Robertson, Gary D. "North Carolina Officials Sought to Charge Political Operator." Associated Press. December 19, 2018. https://apnews.com/58695ada638841e58b8392e3c1d68528

186 Kane, Dan and Portillo, Ely. "'The Guru of Bladen County' Is at the Center of NC's Election Troubles." The News & Observer. April 23, 2019. https://www.newsobserver.com/news/politics-government/article222806255.html

187 Stracqualuris, Veronica; Gallagher, Dianne and Sullivan, Kate. "North Carolina elections board votes for new election in congressional race." CNN. February 21, 2019. https://www.cnn.com/2019/02/21/politics/mark-harris-son-north-carolina-9th-district-hearing/index.html

188 von Spakovsky, Hans. "Four Stolen Elections: The Vulnerabilities of Absentee and Mail-In Ballots." The Heritage Foundation. July 16, 2020. https://www.heritage.org/election-integrity/report/four-stolen-elections-the-vulnerabilities-absentee-and-mail-ballots

189 Caldwell, Leigh Ann. "Republican candidate's son shakes up North Carolina hearing with surprise testimony." NBC News. February 20, 2019. https://www.nbcnews.com/politics/elections/republican-candidate-s-son-shakes-north-carolina-hearing-surprise-testimony-n973836

190 Huey-Burns, Caitlin and Bidar, Musadiq. "What is ballot harvesting, where is it allowed and should you hand your ballot to a stranger?" CBS News. September 1, 2020. https://www.cbsnews.com/news/ballot-harvesting-collection-absentee-voting-explained-rules/

191 Ibid.

192 von Spakovsky, Hans. "Vote Harvesting: A Recipe for Intimidation, Coercion, and Election Fraud." The Heritage Foundation. October 8, 2019. https://www.heritage.org/election-integrity/report/vote-harvesting-recipe-intimidation-coercion-and-election-fraud

193 Eggers, Eric. "Ballot Fraud, American-Style…and Its Bitter Harvests." RealClearInvestigations. December 13, 2018. https://www.realclearinvestigations.com/articles/2018/12/12/ballot_fraud_american-style_and_its_bitter_harvests.html

194 O'Reilly, Andrew. "Ballot harvesting bounty: How Dems apparently used election law change to rout California Republicans." Fox News. December 4, 2018. https://www.foxnews.com/politics/ballot-harvesting-bounty-how-dems-used-election-law-change-to-rout-california-republicans

195 Huey-Burns and Bidar. "What is ballot harvesting, where is it allowed and should you hand your ballot to a stranger?"

196 von Spakovsky. "Four Stolen Elections: The Vulnerabilities of Absentee and Mail-In Ballots."

197 Ibid.

198 Ibid.

199 Ibid.

200 Ibid.

201 Caldwell. "Republican candidate's son shakes up North Carolina hearing with surprise testimony."

202 Huey-Burns and Bidar. "What is ballot harvesting, where is it allowed and should you hand your ballot to a stranger?"

203 von Spakovsky. "Four Stolen Elections: The Vulnerabilities of Absentee and Mail-In Ballots."

204 Press Release. "State Board Unanimously Orders New Election in 9th Congressional District." North Carolina State Board of Elections. February 25, 2019. https://www.ncsbe.gov/Press-Releases?udt_2226_param_detail=229

205 Gov. Roy Cooper (@NC_Governor). Twitter. February 21, 2019. https://twitter.com/NC_Governor/status/1098708571657854976

206 Huey-Burns and Bidar. "What is ballot harvesting, where is it allowed, and should you hand your ballot to a stranger?"

207 Brosseau, Carli; Shaffer, Josh; Kane, Dan and Doran, Will. "Bladen County Political Operative Faces New Perjury, Obstruction of Justice Charges." *The News & Observer*. July 30, 2019. www.newsobserver.com/article233308957.html

208 Doran, Will. "Political Operative McCrae Dowless Accused of Social Security Fraud in New Indictment." The News & Observer. April 21, 2020. www.newsobserver.com/news/politics-government/article242174111.html

209 Robertson, Gary D. "Dowless, Key Figure in NC Absentee Ballot Fraud Probe, Dies." Associated Press. April 24, 2022. https://www.usnews.com/news/politics/articles/2022-04-24/dowless-key-figure-in-nc-absentee-ballot-fraud-probe-dies

210 "A National Map of State Ballot Collection Laws and Ballot Harvesting Prohibitions." The Lincoln Network. September 15, 2020. https://lincolnpolicy.org/2020/ballot-harvesting-laws/

211 Lucas. "7 Ways the 2005 Carter-Baker Report Could Have Averted Problems With 2020 Election."

212 "Section-by-Section: H.R. 1, The For the People Act of 2021." Rep. John Sarbanes. https://democracyreform-sarbanes.house.gov/sites/democracyreform.house.gov/files/SIMPLE-SECTION-BY-SECTION_H.R.-1_FINAL.pdf

213 Dienst, Jonathan. "Paterson City Council Vice President Among 4 Charged with Voting Fraud in May Special Election: NJ AG." NBC4 New York. June 25, 2020. https://www.nbcnewyork.com/news/politics/paterson-city-council-vice-president-among-4-charged-with-voting-fraud-in-may-special-election-nj-ag/2484797/

214 Tully, Tracey. "New Jersey Will Hold Mail-in Election in November, Over Trump's Objections." *The New York Times*. August 14, 2020. https://www.nytimes.com/2020/08/14/nyregion/nj-vote-by-mail-election.html

215 Farrell, Chris. "Mail-In Voting Fraud Growing But Not New." Daily Caller. August 31, 2020. https://dailycaller.com/2020/08/31/farrell-mail-in-voting-fraud-is-growing-but-not-new/

216 von Spakovsky. "Four Stolen Elections: The Vulnerabilities of Absentee and Mail-In Ballots."

217 Ibid.

218 Ibid.

219 "Final Report of the Miami-Dade County Grand Jury." State Attorney Katherine Fernandez Rundle, Circuit Court of the Eleventh Judicial Circuit of Florida in and for the County of Miami-Dade, Spring Term A.D. 2012. December 19, 2012. https://miamisao.com/wp-content/uploads/2021/02/gj2012s.pdf

220 Tanfani, Joseph and Branch, Karen. "$10 Buys One Vote: Dozens Cast Votes in Miami Mayoral Race–for $10 Each." *Miami Herald*. January 11, 1998.

221 Lester, Will. "Court: Carollo Is Mayor of Miami." Associated Press. March 11, 1998. https://apnews.com/article/84166b-4b240a9fbb503b90e8327f5e23

222 "Final Report of the Miami-Dade County Grand Jury."

223 Matter of the Protest of Election Returns and Absentee Ballots in the November 4, 1997, Election for the City of Miami, Florida, 707 So.2d 1170, 1171 (3d Dist. Ct. of Appeal of Fla. 1998).

224 "1999 Pulitzer Prizes." The Pulitzer Prizes. https://www.pulitzer.org/prize-winners-by-year/1999

225 Branch, Karen, et al. "Dubious Tactics Snared Votes for Suarez, Hernandez." *Miami Herald*.

226 In Re the Matter of the Protest of Election Returns and Absentee Ballots in the November 4, 1997, Election for the City of Miami, Florida, 707 So.2d at 1174.

227 "Voter Fraud Issues: A Florida Department Of Law Enforcement Report And Observations." Florida Department of Law Enforcement. January 5, 1998. P. 2. http://www.ejfi.org/Voting/Voting-9.htm

228 Luis Gomez, "What Is 'Ballot Harvesting' and How Was It Used in California Elections?" *San Diego Union-Tribune*. (Republished in *South Florida Sun-Sentinel*.) December 4, 2018. https://www.sun-sentinel.com/sd-what-is-ballot-harvesting-in-california-election-code-20181204-htmlstory.html

229 Re, Gregg. "What is ballot harvesting?" Fox News. April 14, 2020.   https://www.foxnews.com/politics/what-is-ballot-harvesting?utm_source=deployer&utm_medium=email&utm_campaign=weekly%20update&utm_term=members&utm_content=20200424235529

230 Huey-Burns and Bidar. "What is ballot harvesting, where is it allowed, and should you hand your ballot to a stranger?"

231 Wildermuth, John and Kopan, Tal. "California Late Vote Breaks for Democrats. Here's Why the GOP was Surprised." *San Francisco Chronicle*. November 20, 2018. https://www.sfchronicle.com/politics/article/California-s-late-votes-broke-big-for-13432727.php

232 von Spakovsky. "Four Stolen Elections: The Vulnerabilities of Absentee and Mail-In Ballots."

233 Ibid.

234 Lucas, Fred. "15 Election Results That Were Thrown Out Because of Fraudulent Mail-In Ballots." The Daily Signal. April 21, 2020. https://www.dailysignal.com/2020/04/21/15-election-results-that-were-thrown-out-because-of-fraudulent-mail-in-ballots/

235 von Spakovsky. "Vote Harvesting: A Recipe for Intimidation, Coercion, and Election Fraud."

236 Lucas. "15 Election Results That Were Thrown Out Because of Fraudulent Mail-In Ballots."

237 Ibid.

238 Press Release. "Former Mayor of Martin Sentenced to 90 Months for Civil Rights Offenses, Fraud, Vote Buying, and Identity Theft, Press Release, Office of the U.S. Attorney for the Eastern District of Kentucky." FBI. December 16, 2014. https://www.fbi.gov/contact-us/field-offices/louisville/

news/press-releases/former-mayor-of-martin-sentenced-to-90-months-for-civil-rights-offenses-fraud-vote-buying-and-identity-theft

239 "Voter Fraud." The Heritage Foundation.

240 von Spakovsky. "Vote Harvesting: A Recipe for Intimidation, Coercion, and Election Fraud."

241 "SCOTUS Hears Oral Arguments in Ballot Harvesting Case." Republican National Lawyers Association. March 2, 2021. https://www.rnla.org/scotus_hears_oral_arguments_in_ballot_harvesting_case

242 Smith, Ben. "How the Media Could Get the Election Story Wrong." *The New York Times*. August 2, 2020. https://www.nytimes.com/2020/08/02/business/media/election-coverage.html

243 Kim, Catherine. "Poll: 70 percent of Republicans don't think the election was free and fair." Politico. November 9, 2020. https://www.politico.com/news/2020/11/09/republicans-free-fair-elections-435488

244 Bidgood, Jess. "A bipartisan group secretly gathered to game out a contested Trump-Biden election. It wasn't pretty." *The Boston Globe*. July 26, 2020. https://www.bostonglobe.com/2020/07/25/nation/bipartisan-group-secretly-gathered-game-out-contested-trump-biden-election-it-wasnt-pretty/

245 Ball, Molly. "The Secret History of the Shadow Campaign That Saved the 2020 Election." *Time*. February 4, 2021. https://time.com/5936036/secret-2020-election-campaign/

246 Levy, Marc. "Court throws Pennsylvania's mail-in voting law into doubt." Associated Press. January 28, 2022. https://apnews.com/article/pennsylvania-voting-donald-trump-tom-wolf-31b4e7d-0b16a996c63079c8aa3c3b121

247 Editorial Board. "Supreme Chaos in Pennsylvania Voting." *The Wall Street Journal*. September 18, 2020. https://www.wsj.com/articles/supreme-chaos-in-pennsylvania-voting-11600469196?mod=flipboard

248 Bauer, Scott. "Wisconsin Supreme Court disallows absentee ballot drop boxes." Associated Press. July 8, 2022. https://apnews.com/article/2022-midterm-elections-biden-donald-trump-wisconsin-supreme-court-05166e3f3ef970b5cde8ac15cd30e18b

249 Hillyer, Quin. "Wisconsin Supreme Court stands up for integrity of voting laws." *The Washington Examiner*. July 9, 2022. https://www.washingtonexaminer.com/opinion/wisconsin-supreme-court-stands-up-for-integrity-of-voting-laws

250 Research Brief. "Nearly 15 Million Mail Ballots Went Unaccounted for in 2020 Election." Public Interest Legal Foundation. May 2012. https://publicinterestlegal.org/wp-content/uploads/2021/05/Mail-Voting-2012_2020-1P-1.pdf

251 Ibid.

252 Ibid.

253 Ibid.

254 Ibid.

255 Lott, John R. "New Peer-Reviewed Research Finds Evidence of 2020 Voter Fraud." RealClearPolitics. March 28, 2022. https://www.realclearpolitics.com/articles/2022/03/28/new_peer-reviewed_research_finds_evidence_of_2020_voter_fraud_147378.html

256 Ibid.

257 von Spakovsky. "H.R. 1 Is a Threat to American Democracy. Period."

258 Ludwig, Hayden. "How Much Did Arabella's Center for Secure and Modern Elections Undermine the 2020 Election?" Capital Research Center. December 1, 2021. https://capitalresearch.org/article/how-much-did-arabellas-center-for-secure-and-modern-elections-undermine-the-2020-election/

259 "2020 Vision: Reflections on Serving as Poll Workers During a Pandemic." Center for Tech and Civic Life. March 17, 2021. https://www.techandciviclife.org/2020-vision/

260 "Center for Tech and Civic Life." Influence Watch. https://www.influencewatch.org/non-profit/center-for-tech-and-civic-life/

261 Ferrechio, Susan. "Election report finds Facebook mogul's 'Zuck Bucks' broke law, swayed election outcome in Wisconsin." *The Washington Times*. March 1, 2022 https://www.washingtontimes.com/news/2022/mar/1/election-report-finds-facebook-moguls-zuck-bucks-b/

262 Ibid.

263 Ibid.

264 Ibid.

265 Office of the Special Counsel. "Second Interim Investigative Report On the Apparatus & Procedures of the Wisconsin Elections System." Wisconsin State Assembly. March 1, 2022. https://legis.wisconsin.gov/assembly/22/brandtjen/media/1552/osc-second-interim-report.pdf

266 Kelly, Joe. "Former Wisconsin justice suggests decertifying 2020 election results." Courthouse News. March 1, 2022. https://www.courthousenews.com/former-wisconsin-justice-suggests-decertifying-2020-election-results/

267 Foody, Kathleen and Bauer, Scott. "Wisconsin Judge Finds GOP Elections Investigator in Contempt." Associated Press. June 10, 2022. https://news.yahoo.com/wisconsin-judge-gop-election-agency-162923398.html

268 Carlsen, Trevor and Dublois, Hayden. "How 'Zuckerbucks' Infiltrated and Influenced the 2020 Arizona Election." Foundation for Government Accountability. March 2021. https://thefga.org/wp-content/uploads/2021/03/Arizona-Zuckerbucks-brief-3-12-21.pdf

269 Ibid.

270 Ibid.

271 Carlsen, Trevor. "'Zuckerbucks' Followed Biden Voters in Pennsylvania." Foundation for Government Accountability. April 8, 2021. https://thefga.org/wp-content/uploads/2021/04/Pennsylvania-Zuckerbucks.pdf

272 Dublois, Hayden and Lamensky, Tyler. "How Zuckerbucks Influenced the Georgia Elections." Foundation for Govern-

ment Accountability. May 24, 2021. https://thefga.org/wp-content/uploads/2021/05/How-Zuckerbucks-Influenced-the-Georgia-Elections.pdf

273 Salaz, Colton. "Wisconsin election audit details numerous problems with the 2020 election process." Just the News. October 22, 2021. https://justthenews.com/politics-policy/elections/wisconsin-election-audit-details-numerous-problems-2020-election-process

274 Pelley, Scott. "Fired director of U.S. cyber agency Chris Krebs explains why President Trump's claims of election interference are false." *60 Minutes*. CBS News. November 30, 2020. https://www.cbsnews.com/news/election-results-security-chris-krebs-60-minutes-2020-11-29/

275 Press Release. "Two Iranian Nationals Charged for Cyber-Enabled Disinformation and Threat Campaign Designed to Influence the 2020 U.S. Presidential Election." Department of Justice. November 18, 2021. https://www.justice.gov/opa/pr/two-iranian-nationals-charged-cyber-enabled-disinformation-and-threat-campaign-designed

276 "Arizona Attorney General Mark Brnovich Letter to Arizona Senate President Karen Fann." April 6, 2022. https://www.azag.gov/media/interest/ag-brnovich-letter-senate-president-karen-fann-re-2020-election

277 Associated Press. "Brnovich: 'Serious vulnerabilities' occurred during 2020 election." *12News*. April 6, 2022. https://www.12news.com/article/news/politics/elections/brnovich-2020-election-had-serious-vulnerabilities/75-8ca6888c-e717-4bc1-8262-eabac101745e

278 Baigert, Laura. "43,000 Absentee Ballot Votes Counted in DeKalb County, Georgia 2020 Election Violated Chain of Custody Rule." *The Georgia Star News*. August 30, 2021. https://georgiastarnews.com/4300-absentee-ballot-votes-counted-in-dekalb-county-2020-election-violated-chain-of-custody-rule.html

279 Brumback, Kate. "Observer: Georgia county's elections messy, not fraudulent." Associated Press. June 16, 2021. https://apnews.com/article/donald-trump-ga-state-wire-georgia-elections-government-and-politics-87bb23d4d9b2ec80a1db715e6bf1c633

280 Ibid.

281 McClallen, Scott. "Michigan charges three women with election fraud during 2020 election." The Center Square. October 12, 2021. https://justthenews.com/nation/states/three-charged-alleged-election-fraud-2020-election

282 "HR 1: For the People Act." Democracy Reform Task Force. https://democracyreform-sarbanes.house.gov/for-the-people-act

283 "Section-by-Section: H.R. 1, The For the People Act."

284 "The Facts About H.R. 1." The Heritage Foundation. February 21, 2021. https://www.heritage.org/sites/default/files/2021-02/FS_199.pdf

285 von Spakovsky. "H.R. 1 Is a Threat to American Democracy. Period."

286 von Spakovsky. "Ensuring the Integrity of Our Election System."

287 von Spakovsky. "H.R. 1 Is a Threat to American Democracy. Period."

288 Ibid.

289 "The Facts About H.R. 1."

290 Adams, J. Christian and von Spakovsky, Hans. "How H.R. 4 Would Let Leftist Extremists at the DOJ Control the Entire Nation's Elections." Public Interest Legal Foundation. July 26, 2021. https://publicinterestlegal.org/election-frontline/hans-von-spakovsky-and-j-christian-adams-in-the-federalist-how-h-r-4-would-let-leftist-extremists-at-the-doj-control-the-entire-nations-elections/

291 von Spakovsky, Hans. "Destroying Election Integrity: The Unnecessary and Unconstitutional John R. Lewis Voting Rights Advancement Act (S. 4/H.R. 4)." The Heritage Foundation. October 29, 2021. https://www.heritage.org/election-integrity/report/destroying-election-integrity-the-unnecessary-and-unconstitutional-john-r

292 Ibid.

293 Ibid.

294 Adams, J. Christian. "House Democrats want to put radical bureaucrats in charge of state elections." The Washington Examiner. August 25, 2021. https://www.washingtonexaminer.com/opinion/house-democrats-want-to-put-radical-bureaucrats-in-charge-of-state-elections

295 von Spakovsky. "Destroying Election Integrity: The Unnecessary and Unconstitutional John R. Lewis Voting Rights Advancement Act (S. 4/H.R. 4)."

296 Ibid.

297 Ibid.

298 White House Press Release. "White House Announces Additional Staff." March 5, 2021. https://www.whitehouse.gov/briefing-room/statements-releases/2021/03/05/white-house-announces-additional-policy-staff/

299 "K. Sabeel Rahman." Demos. https://www.demos.org/k-sabeel-rahman

300 "K. Sabeel Rahman." Influence Watch. https://www.influencewatch.org/person/k-sabeel-rahman/

301 Biden Administration Executive Office of the President. Influence Watch. https://www.influencewatch.org/government-agency/biden-administration-executive-office-of-the-president/

302 "Demos." Influence Watch. https://www.influencewatch.org/non-profit/demos/

303 "Demos." Discover the Networks. https://www.discoverthenetworks.org/organizations/demos

304 "Demos." Influence Watch.

305 Ibid.

306 Lucas, Barbara Joanna. "Unabashed Radicals: The mission of Demos, Elizabeth Warren's favorite left-wing group." Capital Research Center. July 3, 2014. https://capitalresearch.org/article/ot/

307 "Demos." Discover the Networks.

308 Ibid.

309 Lucas. "Unabashed Radicals: The mission of Demos, Elizabeth Warren's favorite left-wing group."

310 Ibid.

311 Policy Brief. "Executive Action to Advance Democracy: What the Biden-Harris Administration and the Agencies Can Do to Build a More Inclusive Democracy." Demos. December 3, 2020. https://www.demos.org/policy-briefs/executive-action-advance-democracy-what-biden-harris-administration-and-agencies-can

312 "Executive Order on Promoting Access to Voting." The White House. March 7, 2021. https://www.whitehouse.gov/briefing-room/presidential-actions/2021/03/07/executive-order-on-promoting-access-to-voting/

313 "Vanita Gupta." Influence Watch. https://www.influencewatch.org/person/vanita-gupta/

314 Ibid.

315 "Kristen Clarke." Influence Watch. https://www.influencewatch.org/person/kristen-clarke/

316 Adams, J. Christian. "The Left Owns the Election Law Industry." *Frontpage Magazine.* August 11, 2011. https://archives.frontpagemag.com/fpm/left-owns-election-law-industry-j-christian-adams/

317 "Kristen Clarke." Influence Watch.

318 Press Release. "Justice Department Files Lawsuit Against the State of Georgia to Stop Racially Discriminatory Provisions of New Voting Law." Department of Justice. June 25, 2021. https://www.justice.gov/opa/pr/justice-department-files-lawsuit-against-state-georgia-stop-racially-discriminatory

319 Press Release. "Justice Department Files Lawsuit Against the State of Texas to Protect Voting Rights." Department of Justice. November 4, 2021. https://www.justice.gov/opa/pr/justice-department-files-lawsuit-against-state-texas-protect-voting-rights

320 Press Release. "Justice Department Releases Guide to State Voting Rules That Apply After Criminal Convictions." Department of Justice. May 20, 2022. https://www.justice.gov/opa/pr/justice-department-releases-guide-state-voting-rules-apply-after-criminal-convictions

321 Policy Brief. "Executive Action to Advance Democracy: What the Biden-Harris Administration and the Agencies Can Do to Build a More Inclusive Democracy."

322 "Executive Order on Promoting Access to Voting." The White House. March 7, 2021. https://www.whitehouse.gov/briefing-room/presidential-actions/2021/03/07/executive-order-on-promoting-access-to-voting/

323 Policy Brief. "Executive Action to Advance Democracy: What the Biden-Harris Administration and the Agencies Can Do to Build a More Inclusive Democracy."

324 "Justin Levitt." Influence Watch. https://www.influencewatch.org/person/justin-levitt/

325 Ibid.

326 Ibid.

327 Ibid.

328 Ibid.

329 Ibid.

330 Policy Brief. "Executive Action to Advance Democracy: What the Biden-Harris Administration and the Agencies Can Do to Build a More Inclusive Democracy."

331 Letter from Members of House Election Integrity Caucus to Office of Management and Budget Acting Director Shalanda Young. Rep. Ted Budd Website. January 19, 2022. https://budd.house.gov/uploadedfiles/budd_letter_to_omb_on_voting_eo.pdf

332 "A Review of the Operations of the Voting Section of the Civil Rights Division." Office of the Inspector General Oversight and Review Division. March 2013. https://oig.justice.gov/reports/2013/s1303.pdf

333 Ibid.

334 Ibid.

335 Ibid.

336 Ibid.

337 Ibid.

338 "Restoring the Voting Right Act: Combatting Discriminatory Abuses: Hearing before the Senate Judiciary Committee." Subcommittee on the Constitution, Statement of Maureen S. Riordan. September. 22, 2021. https://www.judiciary.senate.gov/imo/media/doc/Riordan%20Testimony.pdf

339 "About Selena Montgomery." Selena Montgomery. https://selenamontgomery.com

340 Brest, Mike. "Stacey Abrams Maintains That She Won Gubernatorial Election." Daily Caller. March 15, 2019. https://dailycaller.com/2019/03/15/stacey-abrams-georgia-election/

341 Ibid.

342 Greenwood, Max. "Abrams launches 'Fair Count' nonprofit ahead of 2020 census." The Hill. March 25, 2019. https://thehill.com/homenews/campaign/435598-abrams-launches-nonprofit-ahead-of-2020-census

343 Markay, Lachlan. "Stacey Abrams Takes Step Towards Running Again by Retooling Dark-Money Group." Daily Beast. January 24, 2019. https://www.thedailybeast.com/stacey-abrams-retools-her-dark-money-group?ref=author

344 Casiano, Louis. "Dem Stacey Abrams still not conceding defeat, claims GOP stole Georgia election." Fox News. April 4, 2019. https://www.foxnews.com/politics/stacey-abrams-refuses-to-accept-georgia-gubernatorial-election-results-says-republicans-stole-election

345 Shaw, Adam. "Stacey Abrams again claims she won Georgia governor's race: 'I'm not' a good sport." Fox News. May 4, 2019. https://www.foxnews.com/politics/stacey-abrams-again-claims-she-won-georgia-governors-race-im-not-a-good-sport

346 Goodkind, Nicole. "Stacey Abrams Burned the Georgia State Flag in 1992 to Protest Confederate Imagery and Doesn't Regret It." Newsweek. October 23, 2018. https://www.newsweek.com/stacey-abrams-flag-burning-georgia-confederate-flag-1184153

347 "Stacey Abrams Biography." Vote Smart. https://justfacts.votesmart.org/candidate/biography/67385/stacey-abrams#.XOuS2shKhPY

348 Klepal, Dan. "State contracts aided candidate's start-up." *The Atlanta Journal-Constitution*. March 16, 2018. https://www.ajc.com/news/state–regional-govt–politics/state-contracts-aided-candidate-start/oO8oAmQZyNWhaCf5PsLTiL/

349 Schallhorn, Kaitlyn. "Georgia governor hopeful Stacey Abrams could become first black, female state leader: Who is she?" Fox News. May 23, 2018. https://www.foxnews.com/politics/georgia-governor-hopeful-stacey-abrams-could-become-first-black-female-state-leader-who-is-she

350 "About Selena Montgomery."

351 Galloway, Jim. "A tale of love, regret and the state Legislature." *The Atlanta Journal-Constitution*. July 13, 2013. https://www.ajc.com/news/local/tale-love-regret-and-the-state-legislature/ygImHgfdJ7GwHQ5q8l3TcI/

352 Farber, Madeline. "Meet the Woman Aiming to Be America's First Black Female Governor." Fortune. June 13, 2017. https://fortune.com/2017/06/13/stacey-abrams-black-female-governor/

353 "About New Georgia Project." New Georgia Project. https://newgeorgiaproject.org/about/

354 "Stacey Abrams." Influence Watch. https://www.influencewatch.org/person/stacey-abrams/

355 Niesse, Mark. "Stacey Abrams' Democratic rival casts doubt on voter registration work." *The Atlanta Journal-Constitution*. May 15, 2018. https://www.ajc.com/news/state–regional-govt–politics/stacey-abrams-democratic-rival-casts-doubt-voter-registration-work/gq5WP7iraCxRyQPwFetjcO/

356 Torres, Kristina. "Georgia AG gets 53 forms in probe of voter registration group." *The Atlanta Journal-Constitution*. September 20, 2017. https://www.ajc.com/news/state–regional-govt–politics/georgia-gets-forms-probe-voter-registration-group/MhhTWfqOh3cdkdoTVmwiYI/

357 Schallhorn, Kaitlyn. "Georgia Dem gubernatorial nominee says 'blue wave' will include undocumented immigrants." Fox News. October 15, 2018. https://www.foxnews.com/politics/

georgia-dem-gubernatorial-nominee-says-blue-wave-will-include-undocumented-immigrants

358 Dottle, Rachel; Koeze, Ella and Wolfe, Julia. "The 2018 Midterms, In 4 Charts." FiveThirtyEight. November 13, 2018. https://fivethirtyeight.com/features/the-2018-midterms-in-4-charts/

359 French, David. "Brian Kemp Did Not Steal the Georgia Governor's Race." National Review. November 19, 2018. https://www.nationalreview.com/2018/11/brian-kemp-did-not-steal-georgia-governor-race/?fbclid=IwAR2d9n_PrGWgmMGY0Zn94A-jwW2qIdaH2DcEivBxcv0R79xCy51toraJIO1o

360 Ibid.

361 Warren, Michael. "The Truth About Georgia's Voter-Registration Kerfuffle." *The Washington Examiner*. October 26, 2018. https://www.washingtonexaminer.com/weekly-standard/2018-midterms-whats-the-truth-about-the-53-000-pending-voters-in-georgia

362 Valverde, Miriam. "Georgia's 'exact match' law and the Abrams-Kemp governor's election, explained." PolitiFact. October 19, 2018. https://www.politifact.com/article/2018/oct/19/georgias-exact-match-law-and-its-impact-voters-gov/

363 Martinez, Gina. "Federal Judge Orders Georgia's Brian Kemp to Unblock Thousands From Voting," *Time*. November 3, 2018. http://time.com/5444011/judge-georgia-exact-match-vote-brian-kemp-stacy-abrams/

364 Fund and von Spakovsky. "Voter fraud exists—Even though many in the media claim it doesn't."

365 Niesse, Mark. "Why did some voting machines sit unused on busy Georgia Election Day?" *The Atlanta Journal-Constitution*. November 8, 2018. https://www.ajc.com/news/state—regional-govt—politics/why-did-some-voting-machines-sit-unused-busy-election-day/GEe491hw2FsEAKESx42TYM/

366 French, David. "Brian Kemp Did Not Steal the Georgia Governor's Race."

367 "Stacey Abrams." Influence Watch.

368 Smith, David. "Stacey Abrams on the ticket? Democrat's star turn fuels talk for 2020." *The Guardian*. February 9, 2019. https://www.theguardian.com/us-news/2019/feb/09/stacey-abrams-democrat-georgia-2020

369 Rutz, David. "Abrams Complains Race Was Stolen Through Voter Suppression, Boasts of Huge Turnout Increases in Same Interview." *The Washington Free Beacon*. April 8, 2019. https://freebeacon.com/politics/abrams-complains-race-was-stolen-through-voter-suppression-boasts-of-huge-turnout-increases-in-same-interview/

370 Lucas, Fred. "Fact-Checking 6 of Opponents' Claims About Georgia Election Law." The Daily Signal. March 30, 2021. https://www.dailysignal.com/2021/03/30/fact-checking-6-of-opponents-claims-about-georgias-election-law/

371 Fausset, Richard. "'Large-Scale Reforms' of Georgia Elections Sought in Federal Lawsuit." *The New York Times*. November 27, 2018. https://www.nytimes.com/2018/11/27/us/georgia-elections-federal-lawsuit.html

372 "Fair Fight Action v. Brad Raffensperger." Courthouse News. December 27, 2019. https://www.courthousenews.com/wp-content/uploads/2019/12/Georgia.pdf

373 Hemingway, Mollie. *Rigged: How the Media, Big Tech, and the Democrats Seized Our Elections*. Regnery Publishing. October 12, 2021 Pages 68-73.

374 Elordi, Maireed. "Stacey Abrams' Voting Rights PAC Helped Group That Pushed Voter Fraud Conspiracy Theories." The Daily Wire. February 24, 2021. https://www.dailywire.com/news/stacey-abrams-voting-rights-pac-helped-group-that-pushed-voter-fraud-conspiracy-theories

375 Amy, Jeff. "Once mocked for her shaky personal finances, Stacey Abrams is now a millionaire." *Associated Press*. April 5, 2022. https://www.latimes.com/world-nation/story/2022-04-05/stacey-abrams-millionaire-running-again-georgia-governor

376 Levine, Jon. "Biden insiders slam Stacey Abrams' veep pitch: 'No one takes Stacey seriously.'" *New York Post*. May 2, 2020. https://nypost.com/2020/05/02/the-powerful-female-democrats-angling-for-biden-administration-jobs/

377 Alfonso, Farnando; Rocha, Veronica; Wagner, Meg and Macaya, Melissa. "The latest on Georgia's new law suppressing voting access." CNN. March 26, 2021 https://www.cnn.com/politics/live-news/georgia-voting-restrictions-bill-03-25-21/h_299f-27574b50c49515e01520521768d9

378 Koffler, Keith. "Chris Christie calls out Stacey Abrams for praising NJ law that allows less early voting than Georgia's." Fox News. April 4, 2021. https://www.foxnews.com/politics/chris-chistie-stacey-abrams-georgia

379 "William J. Brennan Center for Justice." Influence Watch. https://www.influencewatch.org/non-profit/william-j-brennan-center-for-justice/

380 "Fidelity Investments Charitable Gift Fund." Influence Watch. https://www.influencewatch.org/non-profit/fidelity-investments-charitable-gift-fund/

381 "Lakeshore Foundation." Cause IQ. https://www.causeiq.com/organizations/lakeshore-foundation,630288847/

382 "Mai Family Foundation." Influence Watch. https://www.influencewatch.org/non-profit/mai-family-foundation/

383 Ludwig, Hayden. "How Much Did Arabella's Center for Secure and Modern Elections Undermine the 2020 Election?" Capital Research Center. December 1, 2021. https://capitalresearch.org/article/how-much-did-arabellas-center-for-secure-and-modern-elections-undermine-the-2020-election/

384 "Bauman Family Foundation." Influence Watch. https://www.influencewatch.org/non-profit/bauman-family-foundation/

385 "Quadrivium Foundation." Influence Watch. https://www.influencewatch.org/non-profit/quadrivium-foundation/

386 "Proteus Fund." Influence Watch. https://www.influencewatch.org/non-profit/proteus-fund/

387 "Loeb Family Third Point Foundation." Inside Philanthropy. https://www.insidephilanthropy.com/fundraising-in-new-york-city/loeb-family-third-point-foundation-new-york-city-grants.html

388 "Marty & Dorothy Silverman Foundation." Influence Watch. https://www.influencewatch.org/non-profit/marty-dorothy-silverman-foundation/

389 "The Howard and Jackie Shapiro Foundation." Cause IQ. https://www.causeiq.com/organizations/the-howard-and-jackie-shapiro-foundation,134331684/

390 "Rockefeller Family Fund." Influence Watch. https://www.influencewatch.org/non-profit/rockefeller-family-fund/

391 "Ford Foundation." Influence Watch. https://www.influencewatch.org/non-profit/ford-foundation/

392 "Fair Fight PAC." Influence Watch. https://www.influencewatch.org/political-party/fair-fight-pac/

393 "Donors to Fair Fight PAC." Open Secrets. https://www.opensecrets.org/political-action-committees-pacs/fair-fight-pac/C00693515/donors/2020

394 Ibid.

395 Ibid.

396 "Fair Fight PAC." Influence Watch.

397 "Donors to Fair Fight Action." Open Secrets. https://www.opensecrets.org/campaign-expenditures/vendor?cycle=2020&vendor=Fair+Fight+Action

398 "Politics." Incite Labs. https://www.incite.org/politics

399 Ludwig. "How Much Did Arabella's Center for Secure and Modern Elections Undermine the 2020 Election?"

400 Ibid.

401 "Peter E. Haas Jr. Family Fund." IRS Form 990. June 2020. Posted on ProPublica. https://projects.propublica.org/nonprofits/organizations/141962681/202121359349302802/IRS990ScheduleI

402 "Peter E. Haas Jr. Family Fund." Cause IQ. https://www.causeiq.com/organizations/peter-e-haas-jr-family-fund,141962681/

403 "The Sarah Min and Matt Pincus Foundation." IRS Form 990. June 2020. Posted on ProPublica. https://projects.propublica. org/nonprofits/organizations/276641409/202131349349101418/ IRS990PF

404 "Wellspring Philanthropic Fund Inc." IRS Form 990. November 2019. Posted on ProPublica. https://projects.propublica.org/ nonprofits/organizations/223692921/202022899349100022/ IRS990PF

405 "Wellspring Philanthropic Fund." Influence Watch. https://www. influencewatch.org/non-profit/wellspring-philanthropic-fund/

406 "Democracy Funders Collaborative." Influence Watch. https:// www.influencewatch.org/organization/democracy-funders-collaborative/

407 "Trusted Election Fund." Influence Watch. https://www.influencewatch.org/non-profit/trusted-elections-fund/

408 Ludwig. "How Much Damage Did Arabella's Trusted Elections Fund Cause in 2020?"

409 "New Venture Fund—For Support Of Trusted Elections Fund." Hewlett Foundation, June 18, 2020. https://hewlett.org/grants/ new-venture-fund-for-support-of-trusted-elections-fund/

410 Ludwig. "How Much Damage Did Arabella's Trusted Elections Fund Cause in 2020?"

411 Ibid.

412 "Democracy For All 2021 Action." Influence Watch. https://www. influencewatch.org/non-profit/democracy-for-all-2021-action/

413 "Voter Registration Education." Instrumentl. https://www.instrumentl.com/foundations/r40-voter-education-registration?page=4

414 "Carnegie Corporation of New York." Influence Watch. https://www.influencewatch.org/non-profit/carnegie-corporation-of-new-york/

415 "Heinz Endowments." Influence Watch. https://www.influencewatch.org/non-profit/heinz-endowments/

416 "George Gund Foundation." Influence Watch. https://www.influencewatch.org/non-profit/george-gund-foundation/

Donation Amount Provided by the Capital Research Center.

417 "Kresge Foundation." Influence Watch. https://www.influence-watch.org/non-profit/kresge-foundation/

Donation Amount Provided by Capital Research Center.

418 Ludwig, Hayden. "Who Are Arabella's Big-Dollar Donors?" Capital Research Center. January 27, 2022. https://capitalresearch.org/article/who-are-arabellas-big-dollar-donors/

419 America Votes. Influence Watch. https://www.influencewatch.org/non-profit/america-votes/

420 Ibid.

421 Ibid.

422 Ludwig. "How Much Did Arabella's Center for Secure and Modern Elections Undermine the 2020 Election?"

423 "New Venture Fund." The Bauman Foundation. https://www.baumanfoundation.org/grantee/119?order=amount&sort=desc&page=1

424 "Grants Database." Democracy Fund. https://www.democracyfund.org/portfolio

425 "Grants Database." The Joyce Foundation. https://www.joycefdn.org/grants-database?query=new%2Bventure%2Bfund.

426 "Center for Secure and Modern Elections." Blaustein Philanthropic Group. https://blaufund.org/center-for-secure-and-modern-elections/.

427 Ludwig. "How Much Did Arabella's Center for Secure and Modern Elections Undermine the 2020 Election?"

428 Ludwig. "Who Are Arabella's Big-Dollar Donors?"

429 Ludwig. "How Much Did Arabella's Center for Secure and Modern Elections Undermine the 2020 Election?"

430 Freedom to Vote Alliance Letter to President Biden and Senate Leaders. Freedom to Vote Alliance. January 12, 2022. https://www.freedomtovotealliance.com/sign-on-letter

431 Ibid.

432 "Small Business for America's Future." Influence Watch. https://www.influencewatch.org/non-profit/small-business-for-americas-future/

433 "Democracy Funders Collaborative." Influence Watch. https://
     www.influencewatch.org/organization/democracy-funders-col-
     laborative/

434 "Voter Rights Action." Influence Watch. https://www.influence-
     watch.org/non-profit/voter-rights-action/

435 "Voter Protection Program (VPP)." Influence Watch. https://
     www.influencewatch.org/non-profit/voter-protection-pro-
     gram-vpp/

436 Ibid.

437 Ibid.

438 Ibid.

439 "Common Cause." Influence Watch. https://www.influence-
     watch.org/non-profit/common-cause/

440 Ibid.

441 Ibid.

442 Ibid.

443 "iVote." Influence Watch. https://www.influencewatch.org/polit-
     ical-party/ivote/

444 Ibid.

445 "Donors" Open Secrets. https://www.opensecrets.org/527s/527c-
     mtedetail_donors.php?ein=464431052&cycle=2018

446 "iVote." Influence Watch.

447 "All Voting is Local." Influence Watch. https://www.influence-
     watch.org/non-profit/all-voting-is-local/

448 Ibid.

449 Collantes, Francisco. "Law Center Launches Voting Rights Insti-
     tute." The Hoya. October 2, 2015. https://thehoya.com/law-cen-
     ter-launches-voting-rights-institute/

450 "Not Who We Are – Donors." Federal Elections Commis-
     sion.   https://www.fec.gov/data/receipts/?committee_
     id=C00623082&two_year_transaction_period=2016&data_
     type=processed

451 "Secure Democracy." Influence Watch. https://www.influence-
     watch.org/non-profit/secure-democracy/

452	Press Release. "Congresswoman Claudia Tenney Introduces Bill to End Zuckerbucks, Safeguard Election Integrity." Rep. Claudia Tenney. July 1, 2021. https://tenney.house.gov/media/press-releases/congresswoman-claudia-tenney-introduces-bill-end-zuckerbucks-safeguard

453	Press Release. "Committee Republicans' Report Highlights How Ballot Harvesting is Ripe for Voter Fraud & Abuse." House Republicans Committee on House Administration. May 14, 2020. https://republicans-cha.house.gov/sites/republicans.cha.house.gov/files/documents/California%20Report%20Summary.pdf

Acknowledgments

Many thanks to The Heritage Foundation and my colleagues at The Daily Signal that have long had a strong focus on reporting on the importance of free and fair elections.

I want to particularly thank Rob Bluey and Katrina Trinko for their support on this project. I express my thanks to Heritage President Kevin Roberts for his forward to this book and support. Also, while not unique to this book, I would like to express gratitude to Hans von Spakovsky, the nation's foremost expert on election law matters. Conversations with Hans, and reading his research, over the years were very helpful in understanding the challenges to honest elections in the United States.

The book is, of course, possible because of the support and guidance from the team at Bombardier Books and Post Hill Press. I want to particularly thank Adam Bellow, who had a great vision for the book, and Hannah Rowan, who was a great editor.

When reporting both for this book, and frequently when reporting for daily journalism, two other organizations played an important role.

The Capital Research Center, with great investigators such as Hayden Ludwig, was extremely helpful in finding the big money funding the voter suppression myth.

Also, the Foundation for Government Accountability, particularly Stewart Whitson, was a big help in covering the fallout of

President Biden's executive order to turn the federal bureaucracy into get-out-the-vote agencies.

Also, I would like to express gratitude to great election integrity watchdogs such as J. Chritian Adams of the Public Interest Legal Foundation and Jason Snead at the Honest Elections Project.

Of course, thank you to my great family, my mom, three sisters, my nieces and nephews, my wife, and while I'm at it, my dog Jake.

Fred Lucas is the Manager of Investigative Projects for the *Daily Signal*. An award-winning journalist and veteran White House correspondent, he has written and reported for Fox News, *National Review*, *Newsweek*, *History Magazine Quarterly*, Newsmax, *TheBlaze*, *Townhall*, the *Washington Ex-*

aminer, the *Federalist*, the *National Interest*, the *American Spectator*, the *American Conservative*, and other outlets. Before going to Washington, he reported on state capitols in Kentucky and Connecticut. He earned his MS at Columbia University Graduate School of Journalism and a BA at Western Kentucky University. He lives in Northern Virginia with his wife, Basia.

Made in United States
Troutdale, OR
04/27/2024